MW01047025

Don't Blame Me —
I'm a Gemini!

BARRON'S

This book is dedicated to
Bea for her Cancerian kindness and to Jonathan for his
Leonine strength

Don't Blame Me—
I'm a Gemini!

Astrology for Teenagers

Reina James Reinstein and Mike Reinstein

Illustrated by Mike Reinstein

First published by Piccadilly Press Limited, London, England

Text © Reina James Reinstein and Mike Reinstein, 1994
Illustrations © Mike Reinstein, 1994

U.S. edition copyright © 1996 Barron's Educational Series, Inc.

All inquiries should be addressed to:
Barron's Educational Series, Inc.
250 Wireless Boulevard
Hauppauge, NY 11788-3917

Library of Congress Catalog Card No. 95-19890
International Standard Book No. 0-8120-9524-3

Library of Congress Cataloging-in-Publication Data
Reinstein, Reina James.
Don't blame me, I'm a Gemini! : astrology for teenagers / Reina James
Reinstein and Mike Reinstein ; illustrated by Mike Reinstein.
p.   cm.
Originally published : London : Picadilly Press Limited, c 1994.
Includes bibliographical references.
Summary: Introduces the twelve sun signs of the zodiac and describes how
the characteristics of each sign can affect love, friendship, school, home life,
and other areas.
ISBN 0-8120-9524-3
1. Gemini (Astrology)—Juvenile literature. 2. Zodiac—Juvenile literature.
[1. Zodiac. 2. Astrology.] I. Reinstein, Mike, ill. II. Title.
BF1727.25R45   1995
133.5—dc20   95-19890
                                                                         CIP
                                                                          AC

Reina James Reinstein and her husband, Mike, live in North
London. She has worked as an actress and a singer and still does
voiceovers. She now works as an astrological counselor. This is
her first book.

Mike Reinstein is an English teacher. He has been a critic for
Melody Maker and *City Limits* and more recently a cartoonist for
the *Guardian* and *New Moon*.

PRINTED IN UNITED STATES OF AMERICA
6789   9770   987654321

Contents

YOU DON'T REALLY BELIEVE IN ALL THAT GARBAGE, DO YOU?

We think astrology began in Mesopotamia (now in Iraq) about 4,000 years ago and eventually spread throughout the Ancient World.

The journey of discovery must have begun long before this with simple observation. The very earliest prehistoric communities would have noted the phases of the Moon, the Sun's rising and setting and the terrifying drama of an eclipse, when darkness fell suddenly in the brightness of the day.

As civilizations developed, scholars tried to define the laws that govern our universe. They eventually connected what they saw in the sky with people and events on Earth—the first astrology.

For a long time, people believed that the Sun circled the Earth. They also believed that the Earth was as flat as a piece of toast so that if you tried to sail to the end of it you'd fall off.

Aristarchus, who lived in Greece about 300 B.C., was the first to suggest that the Earth revolves around the Sun. It wasn't until the 17th century that the idea became accepted as fact. Copernicus, Kepler, Galileo, Tycho Brahe, and other brave astrologer/astronomers all risked ridicule and persecution in order to define the laws we still recognize today. Astronomy, the study of the solar system and stars beyond, had always been developed alongside astrology.

During the 18th century, a powerful new scientific movement diminished the influence of astrology and elevated astronomy as the only valid way of studying space, the stars, and planets.

In the 19th century, astrology reappeared with a new emphasis that was to change our understanding of this ancient knowledge forever.

The old way of using astrology had been to help kings and queens to rule and the state to prosper. The new way was no less concerned with politics and science, but it now included the everyday lives of ordinary people. It gave you and me the tools to understand ourselves better.

Modern astrology is interested in the way we behave, how we feel about each other, and how we can make the best of our skills and talents.

In the next few chapters we're going to look closely at the twelve signs and also explain some areas of astrology that might be new to you.

And is it really true that Scorpios are only interested in sex and that Capricorns are boring?

Date Table

SIGN	SYMBOL	DATES
Aries	♈	March 21—April 20
Taurus	♉	April 21—May 21
Gemini	♊	May 22—June 21
Cancer	♋	June 22—July 22
Leo	♌	July 23—August 23
Virgo	♍	August 24—September 23
Libra	♎	September 24—October 23
Scorpio	♏	October 24—November 22
Sagittarius	♐	November 23—December 21
Capricorn	♑	December 22—January 20
Aquarius	♒	January 21—February 19
Pisces.	♓	February 20—March 20

1. AN INTRODUCTION TO THE TWELVE SUN SIGNS

Scene: It's a graduation party. Loud music is coming from the living room. Sophie and Mark are sitting close to each other on the porch.

Sophie: Great party!
Mark: Yeah.
Sophie: Did you do all the music?
Mark: Yeah.
Sophie: I like your new haircut.
Mark: Yeah.
Sophie: You're not much of a talker are you?
Mark: Yeah…no…yeah…what?
Sophie: What sign are you?
Mark: You don't believe in all that garbage, do you?
Sophie (indignantly): It's not garbage!
Mark: 'Course it is…anyway, I'm a Scorpio.

Despite his skepticism, Mark knows his Sun sign—he says he's a Scorpio. If Sophie knows anything about astrology, she now thinks she's found out why Mark's so silent and she might even be wondering if he's more interested in her than he seems to be. (See Chapter 3!) How right is she? And what's a Sun sign anyway?

SUN SIGNS

The Sun passes through each sign of the zodiac during the course of a year. That means it spends about 30 days in every sign. The approximate dates given here vary slightly from year to year.

BEING BORN ON THE CUSP

This isn't as painful as it sounds. Being born on the cusp means being born on the changeover day between two signs. If you *are* cuspal you'll want to know which sign the Sun was really in when you were born. If you know your birth time, you can find this out from an astrologer or from a computer service (see the sources at the back of the book).

Of course there are advantages in *not* knowing your real Sun sign: you get to choose which daily horoscope you like best; you're compatible with twice as many people; and you can always use "being cuspal" as an excuse for avoiding gym class.

THE FOUR ELEMENTS

Before going any further, and in order to get a better understanding of the signs, it's very useful to divide them into four groups of three. Each group is related to an element and it helps to picture the signs more clearly if we think of how their elements behave.

The elements are

FIRE—Aries, Leo, Sagittarius
Fire's hot, it's bright, it's unpredictable and exciting. Fire can destroy a city, melt steel, or fry a sausage.

Fiery people are impatient, optimistic, generous, and adventurous. They want life to be a drama and every day to be a challenge.

EARTH—Taurus, Virgo, Capricorn
Earth is the ground beneath our feet. It's stable and strong, like diamonds and coal, salt and sand. Earth can build a bridge, make a planet, or grow a banana.

Earthy people are practical, steady, careful, and reliable.

They want life to be rewarding, and they'll work very hard to make it that way.

AIR—Gemini, Libra, Aquarius
Air is invisible, it's wind and breath, it carries sound and seed. Air can make bubbles in a milkshake, uproot a house in a tornado, or help you sneeze.

Airy people think a lot. They're inventive and talkative, restless, and quick-witted. They want life to be logical and interesting.

WATER—Cancer, Scorpio, Pisces
Water is life-giving, thirst quenching. It's icebergs, tears, puddles, and oceans. Water can be a sleepy lagoon, an enormous tidal wave, or a glass of champagne.

Watery people are sensitive, imaginative, moody, and caring. They want life to be emotionally fulfilling.

THE TWELVE SIGNS

The astrological year begins when the Sun goes into Aries in March—this is called the Vernal Equinox. It's spring, a time of growth and new life.

ARIES ♈ (March 21st–April 20th)
This is the first fire sign and the first sign of the twelve—in fact one is Aries's favorite number.

With a cause and a crusade and a flag to wave, Aries loves to go into battle, beat off dragons, and rescue anyone who looks even a bit distressed.

With so much physical energy, this sign needs plenty of room to be exuberant and noisy. It's great at getting things going but not terribly good at seeing them through. It's too impatient to hang around waiting for permission and too independent to need permission anyway.

The symbol's meant to show the horns of a ram, but you may also see it as two blades of grass pushing through the

3

hard ground at the beginning of spring. Aries bursts through any opposition, no matter how tough the obstacles.

The part of the body connected to this sign is the head. Headstrong. Head first. A marvelous leader, Aries excites people into action.

Connections
Name: Aries come from Ares, the Roman god of war
Planet: Mars
Color: Red
Animal: Ram
Metal: Iron
Precious stones: Diamond, bloodstone, and red stones in general★
Plants: Radish, rhubarb, holly, and thistle

★ There's no general agreement about precious stones and their corresponding signs. We've listed a selection.

4

The most unfair thing to say about Aries:
Aries is a selfish brute.

Aries want results NOW! Yesterday's much too late when you've got an idea in your head and fire in your heart. What's the point of being a rocket if you're never going to be ignited?

TAURUS ♉ (April 21st–May 21st)

The first earth sign. Taurus is close to the land and nature. Think how long it takes for a tree to grow—that's how long Taurus will wait for anything that really matters. You could call this being amazingly patient or infuriatingly stubborn.

This sign loves to satisfy the senses with beautiful food, sweet-smelling flowers, soft fabrics, and lots and lots of lovely money.

The symbol looks like the head of a bull, and bulls aren't noted for being submissive. Taurus is very placid until goaded, then you'd better run for the nearest door.

The part of the body linked with this sign is the neck and throat area. A Taurus often has a beautiful singing or speaking voice. This is odd because bulls only bellow, but perhaps other bulls find that appealing.

Connections
Name: Taurus is Latin for bull
Planet: Venus
Colors: Green, blue, pink
Metal: Copper
Animal: Bull
Precious stones: Emerald and diamond
Plants: Rose, lily, sweet-smelling flowers and fruit

The most unfair thing to say about Taurus:
Taurus is plodding.

Taurus doesn't enjoy change and needs plenty of time to get used to any new situation or learn any new skill. We don't think a bulb's plodding because it takes time to grow into a daffodil.

GEMINI ♊ (May 22nd–June 21st)
This is the first air sign. Gemini is inquisitive, busy, and chatty. There are always hundreds of things popping in and out of the Gemini mind, just as bubbles come to the surface in a fizzy drink.

A typical Gemini sentence starts with the words how? why? or where? (e.g., How do planes stay in the air? Where does your lap go when you stand up? Why do I have to grow up?)

This sign is as lively and spontaneous as a small child and

seems to stay that way forever, just like Peter Pan.

The Gemini symbol looks like the Roman numeral for two. This sign might quite enjoy being duplicated so that it could be twice as active, twice as talkative, twice as versatile.

The associated parts of the body help a bit—two lungs, two hands, and two arms. Lungs take in air and send it out again as conversation; the arms and hands allow us to write, use sign language, or wave flags.

One way or another, Gemini just has to communicate.

Connections
Name: Gemini is Latin for twins
Planet: Mercury
Colors: Dove gray, pale yellow, violet, spots and patterns

Metal: Mercury
Animals: Monkeys, squirrels, and everything that flies, especially butterflies and parrots
Precious stones: Beryl, topaz, striped stones
Plants: Airborne seeds, chamomile

The most unfair thing to say about Gemini:
Gemini is two-faced.

Being interested in everything and everyone at once means that Gemini sometimes turns its back on the very thing that was so fascinating a moment before. A receiver and transmitter of signals, Gemini is like a radar dish constantly rotating in space.

CANCER (June 22nd–July 22nd)

This is the first water sign, sensitive and caring. Male or female, Cancer's the ideal mom of the zodiac, always on hand in a crisis with sympathy and a cup of tea.

Cancer, in its careful and cautious way, likes to protect and keep safe all the people and things that it loves. Cancer sees hidden dangers in pocket money running out, in leaving home for a long journey, or in opening the fridge to find a wrinkled carrot and no milk.

The symbol for Cancer is said to represent the breasts, but you may also see it as an overhead view of two people with their arms around each other, having a loving Cancerian hug.

The associated parts of the body are the breasts and stomach which symbolize the need to nourish and be nourished in return.

Connections
Name: Cancer's Latin for crab
Planet: The Moon (not a planet, but it's up there being heavenly)
Color: White
Metal: Silver

Animals: The crab and other amphibious creatures
Precious stones: Moonstone, pearls
Plants: Melon, cucumber, watercress, and rice

The most unfair thing to say about Cancer:
Cancer's moody.

A crab lives in a shell because it's so soft it couldn't survive outside it. If Cancer feels threatened there's only one
place to be—back inside with the door pulled tightly shut.

LEO ♌ (July 23rd–August 23rd)

This is the second fire sign. Fire is always enthusiastic about life. For Leo it's essential that the road ahead be lit by a rainbow that promises a pot of gold.

When the Sun shines, there will be fun and laughter because Leo likes to do things in a playful and affectionate way, but when life clouds over, this sign's brilliant at making a drama out of no-crisis-at-all.

We could think of the Leo symbol as being the head and mane of a lion, king or queen of the jungle. Kings and queens can rule wisely and creatively, or they can just be bossy. Leo has a bit of a struggle with just being ordinary.

The part of the body associated with this sign is the heart, and that tells us a lot about Leo's generosity and warmth. The heart pumps blood to all parts of the body just as Leo tries to encourage and motivate everyone around them.

Connections
Name: Leo is Latin for lion
Planet: The Sun (being heavenly just like the Moon)
Color: Yellow
Metal: Gold
Animals: Lions and all cats, big or small
Precious stones: Ruby, yellow stones
Plants: Sunflower, dandelion and yellow flowers

The most unfair thing to say about Leo:
Leo's a show-off.

It's true that Leo loves an audience. This sign needs to be applauded and adored for its talents. You wouldn't want to keep the Sun in a box, would you?

VIRGO ♍ (August 24th–September 23rd)

Virgo loves to work and does it with the kind of precision and detail that achieves perfect results. Just imagine trying to fit jewels into something as small as a wasp's knee. That's a Virgo kind of job.

The only problem here is that this sign is as anxious and critical as it is hard-working, so it's unlikely that Virgo will ever award itself more than five marks out of ten.

Virgo has particular gifts when it comes to being of service to other people. There's an interest in the body too and in keeping it healthy. Here's the sign that's bound to know if that spot on your nose is a pimple, chicken pox, or something left over from lunch.

One explanation of the symbol is that the loopy bit represents the intestines, which also happen to be the body area associated with the sign, possibly because their shape is so complex and possibly because they respond so quickly to anxiety.

Connections
Name: Virgo is Latin for virgin (and although it sounds contradictory, Virgo is also connected to fertility, growth, and harvest)
Planet: Mercury
Colors: Grays, browns and all quiet colors
Metal: Mercury
Animals: Ants, bees, and all small, furry creatures
Precious stones: Agate, marble
Plants: All grain like corn, wheat, and oats

The most unfair thing to say about Virgo:
Virgo is a fusspot.

Think of what it must be like to walk around with a microscope, a dictionary, sharp pencils, rubber gloves, and a tool kit inside your head. Virgo has all of these and uses them constantly. If you want a job done properly, always ask a fusspot.

LIBRA ♎ (September 24th–October 23rd)

The second air sign. Libra wants everything to be lovely. Stand still long enough and Libra might just turn you into a work of art. However, physical beauty isn't the only thing that matters to this sign. There's also the need to be reasonable and the need for other people to be reasonable, so that in the end everyone gets along with everyone else. See how nice the world can be?

Libra's symbol suggests the cross beam of a pair of scales. Scales weigh or compare things, and this is a sign that likes to show every side of an argument in order to find the balanced view. It's very hard for Libra to get emotional—it's an air sign after all—but it's not a bad thing to have a calm, rational voice in the room when everyone else has got steam coming out of their ears.

Libra is linked to the kidneys. They're in the center of the body and help to clean and balance the blood.

Connections
Name: Libra is Latin for scales
Planet: Venus
Colors: White and black together, pink, blue
Metal: Copper
Animals: Peacocks, turtledoves, rabbits
Precious stones: Coral, opal, sapphire
Plants: Pansy, violet, sweet-smelling flowers

The most unfair thing to say about Libra:
Libra can never make up its mind.

When you can see every possible result of every possible decision, and everything has its good side, and you don't want to be unfair, and it wouldn't be nice to upset anyone, and the blue one's as pretty as the pink one…no wonder it's difficult.

SCORPIO ♏ (October 24th–November 22nd)

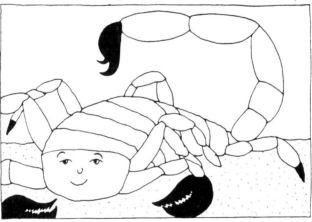

The second water sign. Let's freeze the water and start with an iceberg. Not that Scorpio's cold and lives with penguins but if you really want to find out about this sign you'll have to look below the surface—that's where you'll find passionate emotions, an iron will, and awesome energy. Just like an iceberg, most of what's important about Scorpio isn't immediately visible.

If we think of the symbol as the Scorpion's tail it tells us a lot about how Scorpio can pierce through to the heart of things by finding out secrets and investigating mysteries. It can sting too.

The parts of the body we link with Scorpio are the sexual organs. Yes, the sexual organs, without which of course there would be no new life. In fact, most of the Very Important Things, like sex and birth and death, are connected to this sign.

Connections
Name: Scorpio is Latin for Scorpion
Planets: Mars and Pluto
Color: Dark red
Metal: Plutonium
Animals: Scorpion, snake, eagle
Precious stones: Malachite, bloodstone
Plants: Bramble, blackthorn

The most unfair thing to say about Scorpio:
Scorpio is obsessed with sex.

Actually Scorpio can be obsessed about most things, including not wanting to have anything to do with sex. If it's a serious relationship though, it has to be passionate or it'll be like a bun without the burger.

SAGITTARIUS ⚹ (November 23rd–December 21st)
Sagittarius is the last fire sign, and this one comes with its own set of wheels. On and on, as far as the next horizon, Sagittarius is always going somewhere. This could be with a suitcase and an eternal bus pass, or it could be by learning more and more about everything there is to know about everything. This doesn't mean that Sagittarius is a boring

old fossil poring over books and papers. Sagittarius is actually bursting with optimism and good luck.

The symbol is an arrow aiming at the sky. Even though Sagittarius might not know where the arrow's going to land, there's always pleasure to be had in the flight itself and great expectations that it won't end up point first in a puddle.

The parts of the body related to this sign are the hips, thighs, and liver. Depending on chocolate intake, the hips and thighs are usually the largest area of limb and help Sagittarius to keep on the move. The liver is the largest organ in the body. This sign loves size and is likely to do everything in a BIG way.

Connections
Name: Sagittarius is Latin for archer
Planet: Jupiter (the largest planet in the solar system)
Color: Purple
Metal: Tin
Animals: Stag, horse, the centaur—half man, half horse
Precious stones: Turquoise, amethyst
Plant: Oak tree

The most unfair thing to say about Sagittarius:
Sagittarius is always restless.

   The world's a very inviting, exciting place for Sagittarius. And with such a promising tomorrow there's no time to waste on a tedious today. After all, if you put a racehorse in a stable for too long, it's bound to get tired of the view.

CAPRICORN ♑ (December 22nd–January 20th)

The third and last earth sign. Hear that ticking noise? That's time being very busy—aging us, changing the seasons, turning seeds to plants. Capricorn is very involved with time and the way we fill it. In fact, it's very hard for this sign to waste any time at all.

The symbol looks like a big, curly goat's horn. Ambitious Capricorn probably climbs as many mountains as any goat while going about its business of searching for success and achievement.

The body areas linked to this sign are the skin, bones, and knees. Bones hold us up and skin holds us in, and without a skeleton you'd be a big soggy mess, on the floor.

Organizing things and holding them all together is something Capricorn does best, whether it's planning a party, running a government, or scheduling homework.

Oh, and we mustn't forget knees. Why knees? Why knot?

Connections
Name: Capricorn is Latin for goat's horn
Planet: Saturn
Color: Black
Metal: Lead
Animal: Goat
Precious stone: Jet
Plants: Blackberry and wild fruit

The most unfair thing to say about Capricorn:
Capricorn is boring.

Being organized and efficient and knowing what time it is could be thought of as boring, but then so could forgetting to telephone, losing your favorite book, and turning up for a date on the wrong day. Capricorn's not boring, it's reliable. Doesn't winter always lead to spring?

AQUARIUS  (January 21st–February 19th)

Aquarius is the third and final air sign. The name Aquarius is misleading because it sounds like a water sign. So why is it linked with air? Aquarius loves space, freedom, and independence. The worst thing you could do to this sign would be to enclose it in a room that, no matter how comfortable, held no promise of liberty.

The other thing you can be sure of with Aquarius is that you can't be sure of anything. It's unpredictable, rebellious, and inventive.

Just to confuse things further, the symbol looks like waves on water, but really it isn't. It's light and sound waves, television, radio, and satellite. This is the technology that Aquarius loves to use to communicate across the planet.

The parts of the body associated with this sign are the calves, ankles, and circulation. The ankles are useful for walking, and circulation is a way of linking the whole body as Aquarius loves to link humankind.

Connections
Name: Aquarius is Latin for water-carrier
Planets: Saturn and Uranus
Color: Electric blue
Metal: Uranium
Animals: Firefly, glowworm, electric eel
Precious stone: Blue sapphire
Plant: Frankincense—a gum from the Boswellia tree

Most unfair thing to say about Aquarius:
Aquarius is weird.

It must have felt weird to most people when it was proved that the Earth went around the Sun or when women fought to get the vote. Aquarius is the wind of change, and sometimes you need to be very unusual to open the door to it.

PISCES ♓ (February 20th–March 20th)
This is the third water sign and the very last sign of all. Pisces is as gentle as a warm bath and as easy to lose as a wet bar of soap. Here's a sign that isn't always sure what the facts are but is very sure indeed of how things *feel*. If they don't feel very nice then—whoosh—Pisces swims away.

Being so supersensitive and romantic means there's an inspired sense of creative magic about this sign. Music, color, poetry, and dance are gentle ways for self-expression.

The symbol suggests two fishes tied in the middle and swimming in opposite directions. Give Pisces a decision to make and you're probably in for a long wait. This sign's much too kind to think of hurting anyone by choosing selfishly.

The parts of the body associated with this sign are the feet, beautiful feet that love to dance. They carry the whole weight of the body, and Pisces can sometimes try to carry all

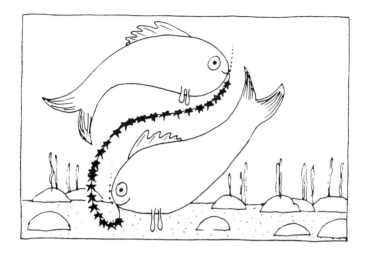

the world's troubles.

Connections
Name: Pisces is Latin for fish
Planets: Jupiter and Neptune
Color: Sea green
Metal: Tin
Animals: Fish and all sea creatures
Precious stone: Amethyst
Plants: Seaweed, water lily, poppy

The most unfair thing to say about Pisces:
Pisces can't say no.

No sign is more aware that the world is full of people needing help and love. Pisces could no more turn away from a friend in trouble than deny a thirsty child a glass of water.

So, there they are, the twelve building blocks of astrology. You've probably recognized yourself in more than one sign. Does this mean that astrology's a load of trash? No. In the next chapter we describe how real astrology works and why people born in the same birth sign are often enormously different.

2. HOW IT REALLY WORKS

An astrological chart or horoscope describes the sky at a particular moment in time and space. It can be drawn up to describe any new beginning, like the launching of a ship, the start of a relationship, the first night of a play, or—most important of all—the birth of a baby. The time, date, and place of the beginning are used to calculate the exact positions of the signs and planets.

Unless two people are born at exactly the same time and in exactly the same town, each birth chart will be different and individual. Two people with *exactly* the same chart are called time-twins. It's highly unlikely that you'll ever meet yours, but there'd be a lot to talk about if you did!

TWINS

Real twins are usually born within quite a short time of each other but even a difference of a few minutes can sometimes make significant changes to a birth chart. If their charts are quite similar then it often happens that each twin will make use of different qualities in the chart during their lifetimes.

MAKING THE MOST OF WHO WE ARE

So many things affect our personalities. We're all influenced by where we live, the people we live with, being rich or being poor, religion, education, what we look like and how healthy we are. And there's always that mysterious something called spirit or soul.

A birth chart describes potential. One of the special things about astrology is the way we can use it to explore our gifts and relate more easily to each other.

THINGS YOU NEED TO KNOW

Apart from the twelve signs and the four elements there are some other vital components that make up a birth chart.

THE PLANETS
(Although the Sun and Moon aren't planets they're always included for simplicity.)

The planets all move at very different speeds. The Moon takes a brisk twenty-eight days to journey through the twelve signs, while Pluto does the same trip at a slow crawl and takes 248 *years*.

Because the planets are constantly changing position, no daily sky will be like any other and every chart reflects these moving patterns. Let's look at the basic meanings for each planet.

The Sun The heart of the chart—so powerful that Sun sign astrology really can describe a great deal about you. It's your true self and the essence of your identity. It's one of the ways to describe how you relate to your father and how he relates to you.

The Moon The emotions. How you show your feelings and respond to situations instinctively. How you care for others and want to be cared for yourself. It's one of the ways to describe how you relate to your mother and how she relates to you.

Mercury Communication. How you use your mind, move and express yourself.

Venus Relationships and possessions. How you love, feel attractive, and appreciate beauty and harmony. The kind of woman you're attracted to and how a woman feels about her femininity.

Mars Energy. How you get what you want, take the initiative, feel strong. The kind of man you're attracted to and how a man feels about his masculinity.

Jupiter Growth. How you use opportunity, increase knowledge, feel joy.

Saturn Control. How you discipline yourself and take on responsibility. Restrictions and defenses.

Uranus Change. How you find freedom, break the rules, show how different you are.

Neptune Sensitivity. How you respond to anything artistic or spiritual. How you yearn for perfection, feel inspired, or try to escape.

Pluto Rebirth. How you let go of what you no longer need in order to make room for new beginnings.

Each sign has particular characteristics and each planet has particular drives or needs that must be expressed.

For instance, the Moon shows your emotional needs and your drive to care for others. If you have the Moon in caring Cancer, then you'll need to feel emotionally secure. You'll look after other people in a very nurturing, caring way.

If you have the Moon in practical Taurus then you'll want to feel that your physical needs are being met before you can be emotionally comfortable. You'll care for people in a very down-to-earth, sensible way.

Quite often, the different combinations of planets and signs in our birth charts suggest that we're struggling to express several very different needs at once—like trying to run in two directions at the same time!

Suppose your chart has the Sun in Capricorn and Mars in Sagittarius. You might find it hard to understand why you're not a typically cautious Capricorn—that dynamic Mars in restless Sagittarius would be urging you to travel and take risks in order to get what you want. Or you might have the Sun in freedom-loving Aquarius and be seriously puzzled about your mad urge to have five children and live in a country cottage. Perhaps you've got the Moon in family-loving Cancer?

ASPECTS

When two planets are a specific number of degrees apart in the sky, the relationship they make is called an aspect. For example, if the planets are between 172°–188° apart, they're said to be in *opposition*. If they're 0°–8° apart, they're said to be in *conjunction*.

There are quite a few aspects and each has a particular flavor to add to the chart, depending on the nature of the aspect and the planets involved.

If we look at Whitney Houston's chart (we'll examine it more closely later in the chapter), we can see that Mercury, the planet of communication, is in conjunction with Uranus, the planet of change and independent behavior. They're both in critical, hard-working Virgo.

That tells us that she communicates inventively, can be inspired to do things in an unusual way, and knows her own mind, particularly when it comes to the way she wants things done.

If the aspect between Mercury and Uranus had been an opposition (which is rather more difficult to deal with because the planets are confronting each other across the chart), then she might have been rebellious and cranky—wanting to do things *this* way because she'd been told to do them *that* way!

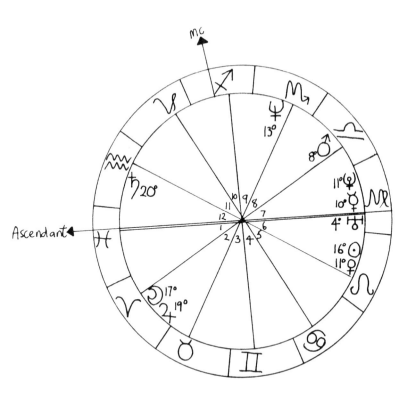

Whitney Houston's Birth Chart

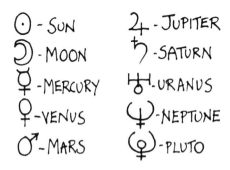

⊙ - SUN   ♃ - JUPITER
☽ - MOON   ♄ - SATURN
☿ - MERCURY   ♅ - URANUS
♀ - VENUS   ♆ - NEPTUNE
♂ - MARS   ♇ - PLUTO

The numbers in the center of
the circle indicate the Houses

THE HOUSES

We've looked at how a planet's principles are affected by the sign it's in and the aspects it makes, but that doesn't tell you whether you'll be experiencing the results at home, at school, or in the way you make friends.

The way to find that out is to divide the chart into 12 sections or houses.

Here's an illustration of the houses and their meanings.

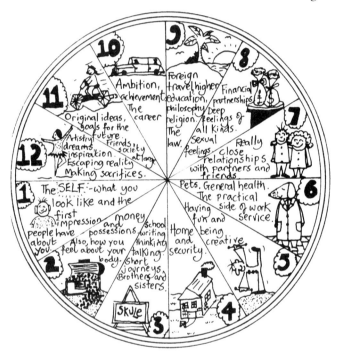

The Houses

Say you were born with Mars in Gemini. This will mean you feel really good about yourself when you're being witty and clever and talking a lot. If that Mars is in the seventh house of relationships, you'll entertain or exhaust your partner with all that endless chat. If it's in the tenth house of career, you might make a huge success of life as a writer or media person.

In Whitney Houston's chart, Jupiter, the planet of growth and opportunity, is in the second house of money and possessions and she certainly has plenty of both to show for all her hard work.

THE ASCENDANT OR RISING SUN

Picture the signs of the zodiac moving around the earth in a huge imaginary wheel. This wheel turns completely every twenty-four hours, so that each sign comes up over the horizon during one rotation.

To make the outer ring of the birth chart we stop the zodiacal wheel at the exact time of birth. The sign that's on the Eastern horizon (the place where the Sun rises each day) at that moment is called the *ascendant* or *rising sign*, because it's rising up and over the horizon.

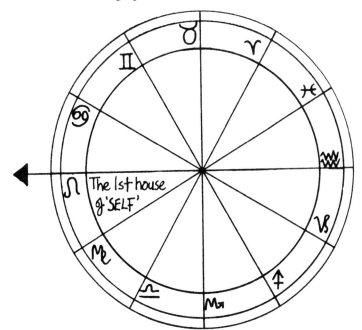

The Zodiacal Wheel of Someone with a Leo Ascendant

The ascendant begins and rules the first house of "self," so that it describes your image, how you're initially perceived by the world, and how you expect the world to respond to you. It's almost like a front office that deals with all incoming and outgoing messages, while the serious business of change and development is going on in another part of the building! For instance, with Leo rising—or running your front office—you'd be quite dramatic and proud on first meeting whereas a Capricorn ascendant would make you much more formal and self-contained.

Back to Whitney Houston. Her ascendant is in Pisces, which means that she comes across as a sensitive and kind person. As we'll see later she's very sympathetic to anyone in need and uses her Piscean love of music to make money for the charities she supports.

THE MIDHEAVEN OR MC

As we've described, when you stop the clock for the moment of birth, a particular sign of the zodiac will be coming over the horizon and forming the ascendant. As the wheel stops another sign will be reaching its highest point in the sky. This sign is called the *midheaven*, which is a translation from the Latin term *Medium Coeli*. You'll be pleased to know that it's usually described as the MC for short.

The MC covers the same kind of issues as the tenth house. Achievement, status, and self-esteem are all connected to this point, so the sign that's placed here on your chart will be a useful indication of the way you want to be recognized and acknowledged for your contribution to society.

In Whitney Houston's chart the MC is in Sagittarius, which shows that she's enthusiastic about her career and eager to learn and explore her potential as a performer.

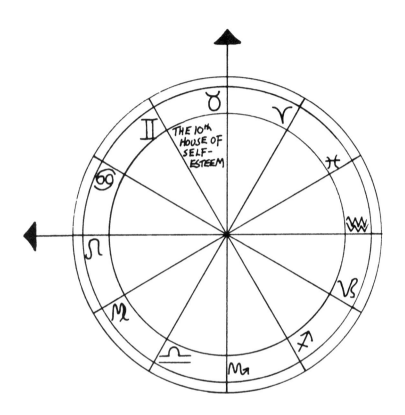

THE 10ᵀʰ
HOUSE OF
SELF-
ESTEEM

The Zodiacal Wheel of Someone with a Leo Ascendant
and a Taurus MC

HOW ASTROLOGY WORKS IN
NEWSPAPERS AND MAGAZINES

The astrologer puts your Sun sign on the ascendant even
though in an actual birth chart your Sun would only be in
that position if you were born at sunrise. With your Sun
sign ruling the first house of "self" the astrologer then
interprets the daily activity of the planets as they move
through the houses and signs and aspect each other.

GETTING TO THE HEART OF THE CHART

All these ingredients affect each other: a sign colors a planet, they both illuminate a house; the planets relate by forming aspects; and bit by bit an astrological portrait is created.

We've looked at a few things in Whitney Houston's chart, and now we'll look at it in a bit more depth and add another famous Leo for comparison. Both these charts share the Leo need for attention and applause, and both people ooze star quality. But even the brief summary we're doing here will show how very different two people with the same Sun sign can be.

WONDERFUL WHITNEY

Whitney Houston has certainly made good use of her Leo Sun. She's the best-selling female singer in the world, has the longest running number one single of all time to her credit (I Will Always Love You), and is now a successful actress! Her Venus is in glamorous, dramatic Leo as well, so it's no surprise that she worked as a model for a time before her singing career took off.

On her chart, Venus is in conjunction with the Sun in the sixth house of work, and Mercury, Pluto, and Uranus are all together in the hard-working sign of Virgo. Work, work, work—success, success, success.

She's probably very good at assessing her achievements too, with that critical Mercury in Virgo making sure that she's the first to spot any mistakes—her own and other people's.

The Sun in the sixth house of service, coupled with that selfless Piscean ascendant, gives us a clue about a rather different side to this megastar.

In 1989 she set up a foundation to help children who are ill, homeless, abused, or in need of educational help. She's a hardworking fund raiser, and with her caring Moon in crusading Aries, obviously likes to fight on behalf of the underprivileged. That Aries Moon sits comfortably in the second house where it can best be used to gather dollars for any needy cause.

How does Whitney get results? Dynamic Mars is in reasonable Libra, so she's likely to use diplomacy and charm. However, that fiery conjunction of the Moon and Jupiter in Aries might encourage her to be quite pushy and impatient under pressure.

And what about love? Mars, the planet that describes the kind of man she'd be attracted to, is in beauty-conscious Libra, so she'll never fall for less than Mr. Gorgeous.

He'll have to be clever though. With Virgo ruling the seventh house of relationships and communicative Mercury sitting in there too, there's a great need for conversation and intellectual companionship.

MR. UNIVERSE

Now let's look at Leo number two. Arnold Schwarzenegger. He's been voted Mr. Universe and Mr. Olympia several times and was generally known for his muscles long before he was noted for anything else. His Leo Sun is in the first house of self, and that's rather a good place for it to be if you're trying to make yourself the biggest thing ever on two legs.

It's hard work getting strong, and conscientious Saturn is right there in conjunction with the Sun encouraging him to be disciplined about training and serious about his goals. His Moon's in cautious, business-loving Capricorn, so he feels a lot safer when he's avoiding risky ventures that might lose him money or prestige. As an extra safety measure, he studied economics in college, while his film career was in its early stages, and developed his skills as a financier.

Back to the first house—it's bursting at the seams with different "selves" that he can call on to suit the moment: there's Cancer on the ascendant, sensitive, careful, and kind; sweet Venus dispensing gentle charm and good looks; the

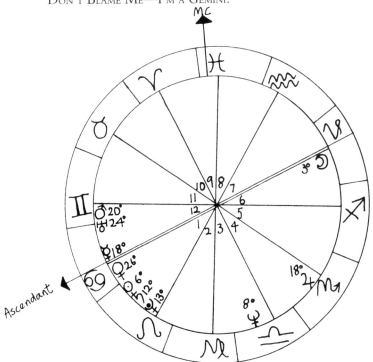

Arnold Schwarzenegger's Birth Chart

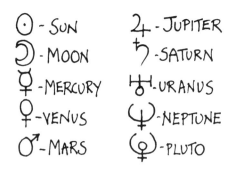

The numbers in the center of
the circle indicate the Houses

Sun being charismatic and creative; Saturn as the strict disciplinarian; and powerful Pluto making sure he knows when it's time to change direction and make the most of his talents.

And energy? Mars of course, and oddly enough it's in Gemini, the sign of the intellect. This is a very clever man who feels as confident about using his mind as he does about developing his body. The explosively dynamic duo of Mars and unpredictable Uranus creates almost superhuman bursts of energy—what a good aspect for The Terminator!

When it comes to love the picture's very different. Venus describes the kind of woman he's attracted to, and with Venus in sensitive Cancer she'd have to be gentle and caring, almost motherly in her willingness to look after him and provide security. Capricorn rules the seventh house so he needs a very traditional relationship there too, steady, practical, and good for his prestige.

We could take thousands of other Leos and look at their charts and be astonished at the differences but equally astonished at the similarities. The Sun's the beating heart of any chart, which is why we can spend the rest of this book looking at the things that people of the same Sun sign have in common.

We know that the world's population can't be neatly divided into twelve giant heaps, but Sun signs work because they're powerful and we recognize their influence in our daily lives.

Let's start with love and friendship and who we like and who likes us, and why.

3. LOVE AND FRIENDSHIP

IMPORTANT PRELIMINARY NOTE

"WHAT SUN SIGN AM I COMPATIBLE WITH?"
This question is actually impossible to answer even though it's asked as often as "What's the time?" or "Where's my other sock?".

For instance, if your Sun sign is Pisces, then theoretically you'll get along best of all with the other water signs, Scorpio and Cancer. You should also be comfortable with earthy Taurus and Capricorn but will feel terribly flustered by impatient Aries and rejected by cool Aquarius.

But WAIT!

Suppose, gentle Pisces, that your Moon is in Aries or your Venus in Aquarius? You might actually feel quite good being around someone who relates to that side of your nature.

There are millions of happy people who should never have gotten together according to Sun sign compatibility, so never say no to a new friendship because someone's got the "wrong" birthday for you.

A SUN SIGN CAN STILL TELL YOU A LOT.
Because it's the heart of the chart, your Sun sign and the Sun signs of the people you care about can still give you real insight into what those hearts need to feel special, even though they don't tell 100 percent of the story.

ARIES

ARIES FRIENDSHIP

You come fully equipped with a white horse and a sword, Aries. At the slightest hint of bullying or prejudice you're in there like a dragon-slayer, fighting for justice and fair play. You're not so keen on listening to people with long-term problems, though, and you'll find it hard to support anyone who seems to be stuck in a situation they can't or don't want to change. From your point of view, a problem that doesn't have a solution isn't a problem at all—so why worry about it?

You won't be shy about making conversation, but it can sometimes be a bit one-sided. Check out any friends who are dozing off when you're in full flow—perhaps they'd like a turn as well? You're not really being rude, but it's hard for you to imagine anyone not being as excited by your experiences as you are.

WHAT DO YOU NEED FROM YOUR FRIENDS?

You want to be with people who are lively and spirited, just like you, and you'd much prefer to floor one of them in a martial arts class than stay indoors and write poetry.

You're an inspiration, Aries, and you love it when your friends get braver by watching you whip your life into shape.

ARIES IN LOVE

When you first see someone you really like—wowee! There's no time to lose and no way you'll be discouraged by your friends.

You're highly unlikely to play subtle little games either, like dropping handkerchiefs or whispering quiet hints about your availability. It's no use if the person you're in love with doesn't know about your feelings, so one way or another you have to blurt it out and declare yourself.

Half the fun is in the chase for you, Aries, and you get the greatest pleasure out of making someone notice you. Once they register your presence they'll probably be so astonished by your fantastically dynamic behavior that they'll surrender completely, and there you are—you've won!

WHAT DO YOU NEED TO KEEP IT GOING?

Because you like to do your own thing, being close to someone can sometimes make you feel a bit trapped and uncomfortable once the initial excitement of the chase has worn off. Your independence can actually be quite scary to anyone who's looking for a more clingy relationship, so it's important to make sure you're with someone who appreciates your dynamism. If you have adventures together, then you won't blame anyone for trying to hold you back, and you needn't feel that love and independence are completely incompatible.

You'll be attracted to quite daring, heroic people but might well find yourself with wobbly, weaker creatures who are drawn to your strength. Take care because you're bound to get bored, and then it's just a matter of time before—wowee!—it's the chase all over again.

TAURUS

TAURUS FRIENDSHIP

Your sweet, open nature's a lovely invitation to friendship, Taurus, but in your earthy way you'll always take things one step at a time.

Once you've decided that you want to be friends with someone and you've settled into a routine, then trains couldn't pull you apart.

Loyal and true, that's you—and possessive too. It's not that you particularly want to own the people you care about, but you'd sooner they didn't do anything interesting with anyone but you. (Or borrow anything you care about for more than twenty minutes.)

The calming atmosphere that follows you around is very comforting and works wonders on wild animals, babies, and friends who have forgotten their math homework, although you do sometimes turn into a sergeant who's drilling a squad into shape. The squad might only be one miserable friend with a cold who really doesn't want to go shopping, but bulls can bully rather well and you won't let your style be cramped for a moment.

WHAT DO YOU NEED TO FEEL COMFORTABLE?

You need to be with people who you can rely on not to be weird or unpredictable. Eccentric behavior makes you very nervous despite your amazing unflappability.

If your friends are loyal, reliable, and warm, they'll find you're there for them tomorrow and the day after that, forever.

TAURUS IN LOVE

You don't speed up when you fall in love, Taurus. It still takes time. That slow, gradual realization that someone matters to you more and more is actually rather delicious, so why rush?

Who's attractive to you? Well, the first place to start is your nose. Your sensitivity to smell isn't far short of a police dog's, so the one you love had better smell sweet. It doesn't have to be out of an expensive bottle, in fact a nice, clean, soapy smell will do fine—or even newly cut grass (if you can find a way of sticking it on).

WHAT ELSE IS ENORMOUSLY IMPORTANT?

Stability, Taurus, that's your goal, and love's another way of achieving it. You'll be attracted to people who are calm and dependable. If you're a Ms. Taurus then you won't enjoy going out with someone who never has any money. Mr. Taurus can be quite the opposite—you'll use money when-ever possible to help you feel important and special.

You're the sign least likely to get upset by sexual stereo-typing—Taurus needs time to adapt to change!

You certainly do get jealous though, so you'll need somebody who enjoys being in a twosome, rather than a flirty, flighty type. If your boyfriend or girlfriend wants space, you'll want out!

Sensual, stable, and sweet—doesn't that sound irresisti-*bull*?

GEMINI

GEMINI FRIENDSHIP

Who are you friends with today, Gemini? Whoever it is, they'd better be ready for a bit of quick-fire dialogue. You're such a chatty, sociable person that people generally feel better for spending time with you. You're quite happy to spread your particular sort of sunshine around and love having lots of friends to share your thoughts with.

Because you live in the cool, airy land of the mind, you might sometimes find that your friends are a bit baffled by your lack of sympathy. You're more likely to be interested in why someone's crying than to offer them a tissue and a hug. If they ask your advice about a problem, though, you'll have lots of good ideas and suggestions for them to try.

WHAT KIND OF FRIENDS DO YOU LIKE BEST?

You could chat to absolutely anyone and find it interesting (for a while), but the friends you want to be with regularly need to be inventive and fun and bursting with ideas. You could write a comedy together, astound each other with card tricks, start a newspaper, impersonate celebrities, or play hangman.

Being bored together isn't likely and is definitely not advisable. You're at your happiest when you're talking, so a silent, sullen friend hasn't got a hope. You'll speed away to brighter faces and come up with a thousand more fascinating things to find out before sunset.

GEMINI IN LOVE

What do you fall in love with first, Gemini? For you to be attracted to someone at all, they've got to be entertaining, clever and bright. Bodies are nice, but brains are *fascinating*, and your curiosity is most excited by a brilliant mind. If you enjoy flirting together and making each other laugh, then it's only a matter of time before the bells of "this-could-be-interesting" start to ring, and there you are—head over heels.

You've got an endless repertoire of funny, endearing, amorous things to say, but there can be times when you get so caught up with the idea of love that you can't quite find the passion to match. Jealousy's completely out of order—you don't understand it in other people and you never feel it yourself. So, if you want to get to know the new face in class you won't be very sympathetic if your boyfriend or girlfriend blows a gasket.

41

HOW LONG WILL IT LAST?

The thought of long-term commitment does make you a tiny bit anxious in case you will get bored, but then again, if the person you care about is interesting enough, it'll feel like having a crowd to talk to every day!

You don't need to be reassured by money and prestige or thrilled by emotional storms. As long as you can talk together for hours on end it won't just be a head to head—it'll be a heart to heart.

CANCER

CANCER FRIENDSHIP

You're not a friend so much as a ready-made family. You need to be needed, Cancer, and anyone who tells you how necessary you are to them is going to win a special place in your life.

One of your specialties is a speedy withdrawal into your crabshell, with claws snapping. Why disappear? A friend might have mentioned, in a casual sort of way, that you seem to have put on a bit of weight. Or maybe someone you like a lot forgot your birthday. Whatever the reason, you'll pop out of your shell when you're good and ready, smile your lovely smile, and wonder why on earth your friends look so bewildered. You've got a cool hand that'll help a headache, Cancer, and a loving cuddle ready to mend a broken heart.

WHAT DO YOU NEED IN RETURN?

Lots of tender, loving care and tolerance of your mood swings might do for a start—you're ruled by the Moon after all and you change faces more often than she does.

It's not all roses being so hypersensitive, wouldn't you agree? Don't let insecurity make you crabby or clingy. The friends you care for really want to do the same for you, so ask them into your shell and tell them what you're feeling.

CANCER IN LOVE
When you fall in love, Cancer, you'll twine yourself around your heart's desire until your heart's desire realizes it can't survive without you. If you want to be happy and enjoy what happens next then remember three of the most important words in your vocabulary: Shelter, Safety, and Security. You're so keen on these three S's that you'll even stay in a relationship you're fed up with rather than be caught off-guard by any nasty, new surprises.

The more anxious you get, the more clingy you get, and there's nothing a shadow could teach you about sticking to someone when you're in full swing.

Celebrating important anniversaries gives you a chance to access your enormous emotional filing system. You can make a romantic milestone out of remembering The First Star Trek We Watched Together.

Other people have memories, but you have total recall and you'll use it shamelessly in an argument. You never throw anything away, and there's probably a box of letters, tickets, photographs, and mysterious dried things in the cupboard to prove how accurate you can be.

WHAT DO YOU NEED TO HELP YOU FEEL SAFE?

That soft, squishy bit that hides away inside your capable, defensive shell is longing to be protected and cared for, so you'd better make sure your beloved isn't cynical, cool, or madly independent. You need a tender, sympathetic soul who can cope with your vulnerability and who'll enjoy being looked after as much as you do.

LEO

LEO FRIENDSHIP

Do you sometimes think of your friends as subjects, Leo, and you as the ruling monarch?

When you slip on your bossy boots there's no way anyone's going to be allowed to interfere with your master plan. They probably wouldn't want to anyway as it's bound to be fun and full of good ideas, but you could probably compromise occasionally without having to surrender your crown.

You've got a fantastic sense of humor, but you really *hate* it when the laugh's on you. Anyone who tries to make you look silly won't be a friend for long but you'll be eternally bonded to the friends who appreciate your limitless talents and superb personality traits. (And you're a sucker for flattery.)

WHAT DO YOU LOOK FOR IN A LOYAL FRIEND?

Because your heart's as big as a palace, you're never petty or mean-spirited, and you could never be close to anyone who adds up kindnesses or gives you presents that cost *exactly* what you spent on them.

Most of us like money but you take a particular pleasure in making grand, generous gestures. If you're broke you might feel powerless, but your real friends won't be true to you because of what you've bought them—they'll love you for yourself!

Find friends you can be whole-hearted and starry-eyed with, Leo. When you're feeling truly confident you radiate a golden glow that'll inspire anyone who's in the spotlight at your side.

LEO IN LOVE

If you spotted a possible new, true love one sunny Sunday afternoon, what would you do? Shrink into the crowd and look longingly from afar? Not likely. Given half a chance you'd probably organize a film crew and make sure your intended got a front row seat to watch you in your big scene. How could anyone resist you when you're looking so good?

Let's hope your intended doesn't turn out to be less than extra special. If your friends think you've gone mad and opened a Charity for Idiots then it'll last as long as it takes to say goodbye. Loyal as you are, you need to be proud of who you're with and can't bear the idea of having to apologize for someone even if you know they're really nice inside.

Actually that pride of yours won't let you be humiliated in any way, even by a Very Special Person, so you won't cope politely if you're ever ignored or insulted in public (or in private).

WHAT MAKES YOU FEEL GOOD?

Love has a funny way of meaning drama in your vocabulary, and if you get masses of affection and attention you'll do everything you can to make your relationship magical, romantic, and larger than life.

You won't be happy with a pessimistic wet blanket who's embarrassed by your vitality and frightened of your enthusiasm, so you'd better look for an optimist who'll laugh at your jokes, applaud your appetite for life, and cherish your big, bright lion heart.

VIRGO

VIRGO FRIENDSHIP

How about drawing up a list of your current friends, Virgo? Making lists is one of your favorite ways to relax, so while you're at it, you could catalog all their good and bad points, decide who you'd like to know better and cross off the people who are always late, vague, or stodgy.

You're so thoughtful that you actually get a lot out of your own company and don't need to have a constant flow of friends around you to stave off boredom. The times you choose to be alone give you room to work or be creative or indulge in one of your Gold Medal Olympic Worry Sessions. These can be very absorbing and run on for several days, so this is when a good friend really counts. Pour your heart out, get some advice, and tidy your cupboards until you feel better.

WHO'LL BE ON YOUR LIST?
The friends with high marks are likely to be witty and clever. It drives you bonkers to be around slow, humorless people who get their facts mixed up. Bottom of the list? Friends who try to surprise you, no matter how well-intentioned their motives. Your earthy nature hates being taken off-guard and you get thrown into an immediate tizzy if you feel you've been intruded on.

The friends you get close to will always be able to rely on your intelligent, watchful kindness. You'll never be sentimental and gushy, but your cool, clear logic and pointed wit are gifts to treasure.

VIRGO IN LOVE
How often have you turned your nose up at a potential love, Virgo?

The basic essentials aren't open to debate so no proposals of any kind are welcome unless the applicant is intelligent, tactful, and tastefully dressed. Add a nice laugh and clean teeth, and you might start feeling a bit fidgety and quietly excited.

Being in love doesn't mean you won't find things to criticize and you can certainly be quite picky when you're in the mood. You're just as hard on yourself when it comes to finding fault, and this can all get in the way of the nice things you'd much sooner be doing together.

Seeing what's wrong is the first step to putting things right, but it all depends on how you choose to tell each other.

WHAT DO YOU NEED TO FEEL AT EASE?

You don't like big, sloppy displays of look-at-me-I'm-in-love and much prefer to be cool and dignified in public. You'd never dream of getting involved with anyone who's idea of fun would be to get silly at a disco, show off in class, or embarrass you in front of your friends.

This doesn't mean you don't feel things very deeply. When you're alone with someone you love you'll let go and unwind a lot more. That's when your gentle, considerate nature really comes into its own. Somehow or other (could it be magic?) you seem to know exactly what the other person needs long before they've thought of it themselves.

LIBRA

LIBRA FRIENDSHIP

You're a born diplomat, Libra. If your friends are finding it difficult to understand each other, you'll do everything you can to smooth things over.

You just can't stand the idea of a nasty argument. Having a horrible fight with a friend in a dingy room with peeling wallpaper and dead flowers on the mantelpiece is your vision of Hell. Especially if you're not looking your best. Heaven would be much prettier. You'd be beautiful, your friends would be saying sweet things to each other, and everyone would be smiling and radiating harmony.

On the other hand (remember that, it's a very Libran phrase), although you yearn for peace, you're not averse to having a really sparky discussion. It's all that air looking for ways to communicate.

WHAT KIND OF FRIENDS WOULD YOU LIKE TO HAVE?

You need to do everything in pairs. You want to share your ideas and debate the big issues of life. You're happy to talk about anything as long as it doesn't get too personal and unpleasant and threaten your friendships even a tiny bit. Your friends need to be tolerant, attractive, reasonable, and very, very nice. They'll groan about the weeks you spend trying to make decisions, they'll love the way you're always interested in what they're doing, and they'll never fail to be enchanted by that extraordinary smile.

LIBRA IN LOVE

You can charm any bird straight out of its tree, Libra, so potential partners should be lining up outside your door. Nice as that might sound, it's not the easiest situation in the world for you.

Being indecisive is annoying enough when you're trying to pick a scarf. If two or more incredibly attractive possibilities present themselves, you won't know which to choose and could easily end up being insincere as you try to please them all.

Whoever you choose (if you ever do) they'll have to be quite amazingly even-tempered. Tantrums make you ill, and even a mild display of bad manners can leave you feeling queasy.

WHAT ELSE DO YOU NEED TO BE HAPPY?

Good looks are crucial, buckets of charm are irresistible, and you can never have enough of the sweet things that help to produce a romantic mood, like chocolate and mushy music and moonlight and chocolate and flowers and chocolate.

If the beautiful world of your relationship moves into nasty weather, you'll try very hard to pretend that nothing's going wrong. Bending over backwards to keep the balance may seem like the best solution, but you might bend back so far that you end up looking like a hairpin and lose your balance anyway. Behind those rosy spectacles there's a brilliant mind just longing to make sense of any problems and a gentle, sensitive heart that loves to be in love more than anything else in the world.

Open up your door, Libra, and start sorting through that lovesick line-up.

SCORPIO

SCORPIO FRIENDSHIP

In a crisis, Scorpio, you'd probably volunteer to remove your best friend's appendix on the lab floor. You never go to pieces in an awkward situation. In fact you actually enjoy probing into the dark and secret area of other people's minds. It'll be one-way traffic, of course, because wild horses couldn't drag a squeak out of you if you felt that your secrets might be used against you.

You're quite suspicious of strangers and it takes a while for you to put your trust in a new friend. Once given, your loyalty's cast iron. You'll take your friendship very seriously indeed, even if you find it difficult to say what you're feeling out loud.

If a friend ever betrays that trust, you won't rest until you've gotten revenge. Take care of that sting in your tail, Scorpio. It's probably a lot more painful than you realize, for your victim and for you.

WHAT DO YOU LOOK FOR IN A FRIEND?

A Scorpion wouldn't get too close to a humble, uncomplaining mouse unless it wanted the mouse to be a humble, uncomplaining breakfast. You definitely need strong, fascinating friends who'll match your appetite for mystery and respect your need for privacy.

They'll be drawn to your charisma, complain that you're too stubborn, and know that you'll be in control no matter how tough things get.

SCORPIO IN LOVE

Unless you're very unusual, Scorpio, the first remarkable thing that'll attract anyone to you is your eyes. They're piercing, straight-to-the-heart, and guaranteed to make anyone you like feel very strange indeed.

Of course, no matter how excited you're feeling, you won't let it show. A brass band could be tuning up in your heart, but your cool see-if-I-care face won't betray a thing until you're ready.

Silence is always a handy tactic in your armory. You can use it to suggest that you're struggling with animal instinct and that you only need a little persuasion to explode into an abandoned frenzy. If you're icy with anger, you can use it like a weapon and wither the opposition with a raised eyebrow and a sniff.

You need to be in control, however you decide to do it, and one of the things that makes you feel most *out* of control is being jealous. At the first hint of a threat to your relationship, even if you're still at the "maybe" stage, you'll start to boil and stew. In your all-or-nothing way you want to be the absolute one and only, and there's no way you'll tolerate anything less. So there.

WHO WOULD YOU LIKE TO BE THE ONE AND ONLY WITH?

You take things too seriously for a fluffy lightweight who's scared of those powerful watery feelings. If you want it to last for aeons (and you do), then go for a deep, emotional someone who's powerful enough to look you in the eye without blinking.

SAGITTARIUS

SAGITTARIUS FRIENDSHIP

When was the last time you opened your mouth and put both feet in it, Sagittarius?

Suppose you bump into a friend who happens to be wearing a dress that looks as if it's been stapled together out of old kitchen curtains? You'll probably laugh and point helplessly while your more tactful friends are telling her how sweet she looks in green plastic.

If you find out that you've hurt anyone you always feel awful. There just seems to be a short circuit between what you think and how you say it.

WHO WOULD YOU LIKE TO HAVE FUN WITH?

Rather than laughing *at* your friends, you'd much prefer to laugh *with* them. Because you're always on the lookout for excitement there's no point hoping that you'll make a best buddy out of anyone who's too serious, nervous, or fearful of change.

Every now and again, you'll feel an overwhelming urge to tell your friends exactly what life's about. You'll expect them to listen carefully and laugh at all your jokes (even though you usually forget the punch line). After all, being a philosopher isn't much fun if nobody's taking notes.

You need straightforward, happy friends who won't mind too much when you say awful things about their taste in clothes. Whatever they're wearing they'll want to be your traveling companions as you set off in search of the next Big Adventure.

SAGITTARIUS IN LOVE
When you fall in love, Sagittarius, that arrow of yours comes straight from Cupid's bow.

Sitting on the fence isn't your style at all. You're bold and blunt and easily excited by the possibility of taking a bright new heart by storm.

After the first mad moments when the arrow hits home, you'd better start to back off a little, especially if you feel that you're being restricted in any way. You've got to feel free to come and go, and you're honest enough to say so.

WHO WILL YOU AIM YOUR ARROWS AT?
Anyone who thinks they can sneak into your heart by being phony and devious had better get used to the sound of you running. In the other direction. What you can't resist is a clear-eyed, direct, what-you-see-is-what-you-get person. You might find yourself being attracted to people who are quite worldly-wise as well—people you feel you can learn something from.

Being too close to a sad face makes you very nervous, and if someone you love's feeling depressed you'll probably try to see the funny side of the situation. If you're lucky you'll end up getting a laugh. You might also end up with your very sad friend looking for someone who'll hand over a hankie and listen sympathetically.

Don't be so scared of the occasional blue mood, Sagittarius. Whether it's yours or someone else's, you won't lose your wonderful love of life for long.

CAPRICORN

CAPRICORN FRIENDSHIP

You don't make friends on a whim, Capricorn. With your cautious, practical nature, you'll add up all the reasons for and against and then stop and think again.

You'll be seriously put off if your potential friend decides to sing a very rude song to a nervous crowd while you're waiting for the bus home. In fact, you'll probably walk. Although you've got a wicked sense of humor, public displays of any kind give you goosebumps.

WHAT DO YOU REALLY WANT?

You're much more comfortable when everything's under control and everyone's on their best behavior. You really need friends who are rock solid and safe, and if they're useful as well then so much the better. Mutual cooperation's a great way to make progress, but if you're only interested in someone because you might get something out of it, the friendship's bound to fall apart in the end. If you get a leg up, remember to let down a ladder.

When it comes to remembering birthdays, you're a walking diary, that's just one of the thoughtful, considerate things that make your friends feel valued and special.

If you're having one of your gloomy days, don't bottle up your feelings. Ask a friend for a sympathetic ear and a private cuddle. Then you can get it all off your chest and bounce back to the control panel where you belong.

CAPRICORN IN LOVE

You're not as confident as you look, Capricorn, and you need a relationship to help you feel more secure.

You'll never throw your heart at a stranger in case they drop it with their butterfingers and it breaks into a thousand pieces on the floor. After a while, when you're reassured that there's no danger of rejection or ridicule, you might see that they're actually wearing a giant pair of baseball gloves so your heart'll be quite safe. Then you can get a little closer to admitting your feelings.

Deep down, despite your cool, calm behavior, there's a passionate earthy core. Once you've made a commitment you'll be every bit as supportive as scaffolding (and nicer to hold).

WHO WOULD FEEL SAFE ENOUGH FOR YOU?
Chances are that you wouldn't enjoy being with anyone much younger than you, especially if they hadn't learned to put a proper value on hard work and achievement. You want to be with someone who's mature enough to take you seriously, capable enough to have made the very best of themselves, and quick enough to love your high-speed humor.

You've worked hard on your image (even if *you're* not always convinced by it) and you'll give your heart to the person who appreciates and respects the success you've worked for, but loves the vulnerable you inside.

AQUARIUS
AQUARIUS FRIENDSHIP
If you had time, Aquarius, you'd be friends with the entire population of the world, the solar system, the universe, and beyond.

You're happy to talk to anyone, even if they've got antennae, hairy teeth, and feet like tennis rackets. In fact, the odder and more interesting people are, the more interested you'll be.

Just because you like being with lots of people, it doesn't mean you want to be one of the crowd. Whatever extraordinary new trend you've been inspired to start, your friends are bound to copy it, and then you'll have to run off and experiment with something else.

WHAT DO YOU NEED MOST?

As long as you've got room to breathe, you're the kindest and most helpful friend imaginable, but if anyone tries to get too close you'll do a vertical takeoff and leave them talking to your shoes. With your airy, curious detachment, it's always easier for you to enjoy a group of people than it is for you to get deeply involved with anyone in particular.

It's hard to change the world on your own, so you need friends who care about the human race as strongly as you do. If they're happy to see you when you breeze in and happy to say goodbye when you breeze out, you'll probably be friends long enough to change the world together.

AQUARIUS IN LOVE

You'll always need to think of the person you love as your best friend, Aquarius. No amount of seductive eye contact and meaningful whispering would persuade you into a relationship if you weren't intrigued and excited at a mental level first.

Being pinned down to an arrangement makes you very itchy, especially if it means you might miss the chance to do something unexpected. If you're meant to be somewhere at three o'clock and you're offered a more interesting option at two-thirty, your three o'clock date might well end up making friends with a lamppost.

Whatever happens when you're not there, you won't be drawn into feeling jealous, and you won't like it if your boyfriend or girlfriend gets into a lather about where you've been and with whom and why.

Your great big global heart just can't understand why we can't all be friends. That includes the people you've been out with, the person you're going out with now, and anyone you happen upon in the future. They'll all need to get along with each other if they want to get along with you.

WHAT ELSE DO YOU NEED FROM A "BEST FRIEND"?

Intelligence, of course, and independence because you really don't like being leaned on. The one thing you need more than anything else is space, and you'll offer it in equal measure to anyone you care about. You want the kind of freedom that means you'll only get together because you really want to see each other. Isn't that nicer than habit?

PISCES

PISCES FRIENDSHIP

You don't just sympathize with someone, Pisces, you feel what they're feeling, right down to your toes, via your tender heart. This is good news for your friends, who know you'll laugh with them when they're happy and cry with them when they're sad.

Taking the initiative doesn't appeal to you much. You're so adaptable that you often prefer to be a part of other people's plans, just as water takes its shape from whatever container it's in.

You don't want friends who'll drag you into a boring gray world full of monotonous routine. Wouldn't you sooner live in a land where people dance their nights away on huge shiny floors surrounded by fairy lights and magical music?

HOW WOULD YOU RECOGNIZE A REAL FRIEND?

Reality can often be a bit of a disappointment to you and you might decide to hide away at times when you're feeling particularly fragile and disillusioned. Your true friends won't mind waiting till you feel like meeting the real world again.

The people you're close to should be gentle and sensitive, Pisces. They'll need to be patient when you vanish from view, helpful when you forget what day it is, and ready to join you in that enchanted place where nothing's quite as ordinary as it seems.

How You Can Tie Yourself in Astrological Knots

PISCES IN LOVE

You're always looking for the perfect mate, Pisces. The current object of your fantasies may well be showing no interest in you at all, but that won't stop you from writing poetry during human biology and walking into walls because you're so lost in a sweet daydream.

Ordinary things like pimples and runny noses can get in the way of your fairy-tale expectations, but you'll usually be able to turn the most ordinary date into a special event with your bewitching charm.

Your emotions are really near the surface. Nothing would make you happier than to share your very deepest feelings with a true love.

Sometimes you might fall for people who aren't terribly happy or successful and try to turn them into Perfect Beings. This doesn't usually work out. If they cheer up and do well they might not stay around, and if they don't cheer up you could feel a bit stuck.

If you ever decide to say goodbye, you won't want any unpleasant confrontations—you'll just disappear like a fish in deep water.

WHO'LL TAKE CARE OF YOUR HEART?
If you're going to stay and enjoy yourself you'll need to be with someone who's romantic and vulnerable but strong enough to stand on their own feet, most of the time. When you're feeling a bit chaotic you'll want a caring person there to help you make sense of things, and you'll be just as ready to help out if your true love's having a difficult day.

The real truth is that there's no such thing as a Perfect Being. All you need is a little bit of magic and a lot of love to make an ordinary person very special.

4. SCHOOLS AND RULES

ARIES

IN THE CLASSROOM

By now, Aries, you'll have gathered that you're an independent sort of person with some rather definite ideas about what you want to do and when you want to do it. (NOW!)

You're not, in short, terribly good at following instructions. Given that a teacher's job is to instruct—how exactly are you likely to deal with this potential stalemate?

Even though the curriculum really dictates just how flexible a teacher can be, you'll be far more enthusiastic and ready to work for someone who makes lessons fun and gives you as much room as possible to do things your way, as long as you do it in 45 minutes (you'll do it in 15).

You'll feel much more fidgety with a teacher who likes to do things slowly and methodically. If you get too hot and bothered, don't just bang things on the desk—imagine yourself standing in some nice, cool rain till you calm down enough to get on with what you've been asked to do. Your teacher's probably completely unnerved by the speed you like to work at and can't believe that you could do something so well, so quickly.

SUBJECTS

Any subject that needs patience and attention to detail is likely to have you tearing your hair out, so don't feel inadequate if you're not immediately successful with fiddly things like test tubes and sewing. If it's competitive and noisy you'll have a great time. That means sports get a gold star. Drama is fun. Technology, geography, and sociology are interesting. History's good as long as you can identify with the action.

HOMEWORK

You'll always work better if you're not tense and twitchy through lack of exercise. Live dangerously and draw up a timetable (yuk!) for yourself, so that you can sandwich schoolwork in between nice sweaty bouts of whatever exercise you like best. You're not the neatest person in the world (no time), but you could at least check spelling and punctuation.

STUDYING AND EXAMS

Studying is only difficult because you hate doing anything twice. You think fast and if you whiz through things in your hurry to move on, you're bound to leave things out. This might mean you'll be in a pickle during exams, so never give up after the first read-through.

When you're actually taking exams, make sure you haven't done the paper so fast that you've forgotten to put your name on it. By the time you've checked for mistakes you might still have an hour left to write a play and file your nails.

TAURUS

IN THE CLASSROOM

You're essentially a good-natured, steady sort, Taurus. As long as you're not expected to do things in a hurry, you're perfectly happy to get on with whatever's put in front of you.

If you ever do decide to dig your heels in over an issue then the entire staff, including the janitor, won't be able to change your mind. You're so stubborn that you probably won't even listen to yourself when you realize it's time to give in.

A foolproof timetable and teachers who always allow you to develop at your own speed—that's the kind of atmosphere you need to feel at ease. You're not likely to enjoy working with a teacher who springs a test on you when you're settling down to a nice lesson of private reading.

Give yourself a few minutes to stop thinking about what you were going to do and adjust to the new plan. Try imagining a TV screen and keep changing channels till you get to one that's got a picture of what you have to do now. Good luck!

SUBJECTS

You might not be a star in the sports hall—physical exertion isn't your favorite thing (except dancing, which you love). You're probably an expert at notes to get you out of gym. Have you tried "gophers buried my sneakers"?

Subjects you'll enjoy should include home economics (you can eat the results); business, to help you make lots of money; and anything to do with music and dance. All the visual arts are great too: ceramics, painting, and design.

HOMEWORK

The main problem you face at home is a sort of snoozy feeling that washes over you just as you're sitting down to work. You'll stock up on munchies, watch a video, play with the cat, and suddenly it'll be too late to finish that essay.

When you finally get down to work, you're actually methodical, tidy, and industrious.

STUDYING AND EXAMS

Studying isn't a problem either, once you get down to it. You'll keep reading and remembering till everything's safely stored away and easy to access when you need it. You're usually pretty unruffled in situations that turn other people's blood to water. Exams are no exception. You'll plow through the paper, looking neither right nor left till you put your pen down at the end.

GEMINI

IN THE CLASSROOM

Has your report card ever read "...is easily distracted"? Teachers, on the whole, will try and get you to concentrate on one subject for at least fifty minutes. If you're really involved and excited about something, you'll concentrate effortlessly for hours, but if you're bored, then it's "bye-bye" work and "hello" almost any other distraction.

Because you're so curious and interested in everything, you're actually very easy to educate, except for one major problem: you never stop talking. Teachers don't usually appreciate just how important it is for you to keep your friends informed during lessons.

Being told what to do doesn't bother you as long as you're interested in the subject. If you have to spend ages going over and over something, and it's tedious and mono-tonous and deadly dull, you'll be driven crazy. If your teacher's not having an inspired day you might not feel much like cooperating either.

You're so clever you're almost a computer, so why not imagine you're just programming in some more informa-tion. When the data's assembled you can turn it off and do what you want!

SUBJECTS

You are interested in almost everything, with a few favorites. You love words, so English, media studies, foreign languages, and debating skills are all important. Computers, graphics, and design technology are fascinating, and all sports are fun. Cooking might not be very appealing at first, but the more you know about anything, the more interesting it becomes.

HOMEWORK

Even though concentration's not your strongest point (you can always learn to develop more with practice), you'll work really hard when you're motivated. You could try cutting down any work that's boring into short, manageable chunks of no more than half an hour. In between each chunk you could give yourself five minute "rewards"—a video game, music, take the dog for a walk.

Being tidy isn't as important to you as getting your ideas across, so you might need to get into the habit of doing two drafts when you write.

STUDYING AND EXAMS

Studying is the perfect opportunity to practice half-hour chunks, but if you're feeling particularly studious and hard-working you might like to go on longer between breaks.

In exams you might be tempted to include every known fact connected to the subject, so when, for example, you're writing about the Wall Street Crash of 1929, do not necessarily include intimate biographical details of John D. Rockefeller. Unless you absolutely have to

CANCER

IN THE CLASSROOM

Wherever you are, Cancer, you want it to be a home-away-from-home. A classroom's about as cozy as a traffic jam, but your teachers' would hardly appreciate it if you brought in your pillow and a comfortable chair to read in.

You could always make sure your school bag's got some comforting things to eat and a few photographs of the people you care about in case you need to feel secure. If you've forgotten your bag and you're feeling anxious, why not imagine yourself all wrapped up in a big soft blanket for a few minutes—that should help.

Logic may not be your greatest asset; but intuition definitely is. You can have huge intuitive leaps or hunches that hit the answer right on target. You'll then spend hours working out what on earth you meant. Trust yourself and you'll see just how valuable those feelings can be.

You're not keen on being told what to do. Even if it's justified, criticism will make you hurtle back into your shell to brood. Your ideal teacher is never critical, always calm, and doesn't exist anywhere in the universe.

Find a teacher you really like most of the time and talk about your insecurity. Once you're feeling safe, you'll work twice as hard.

SUBJECTS
You might not get terribly excited about science, especially the gory bits. Geography's mostly about places that are dangerously far from home, and sports can be muddy (except for swimming, which gets high marks).

History's great, particularly when you can visualize how ordinary people lived. Anything to do with food's a winner. Music, dance, painting, and English all feed your wonderful imagination.

HOMEWORK
The first thing to do is make yourself a special place to work. It doesn't matter if you have to dismantle it every time you finish—it might be a tiny corner, it might even be in the library.

Set up a comfortable spot and put a few things in it to make you feel cozy. Once you're in the mood you'll work your socks off and it'll look ordered and neat.

STUDYING AND EXAMS
You might put off getting down to serious studying because you're worried that you won't do well in the exams. This is like saying, "If I put my hands over my eyes the vase I've just broken will disappear." It doesn't work. Try setting up that comfortable place and work a lot more

socks off.

Exams are mostly about remembering vast amounts of information and getting it down on paper before the whistle blows. Memory is one of your strong points. Add an equally vast amount of intuitive intelligence and how can you fail?

LEO

IN THE CLASSROOM

There aren't many situations (any situations?) where you're happy to take a back seat, Leo. School has a few danger areas. You might not be top of the class, you might not be captain of a sports team, and—this is difficult to swallow— you're definitely not a teacher. (But you might be one day—see Chapter 5.)

You enjoy organization and school discipline does suit you very well, but you have to feel that you're being treated with respect and being admired for your contribution to the class.

If you respect the teacher in return, then you'll move mountains to prove yourself. If you're feeling disobedient, you could always try imagining yourself behind the big table in the Oval Office at the White House, surrounded by your aides and visiting heads of state. . .once you're feeling good and special, you should have calmed down enough to do your work without snarling.

Teachers who make their lessons dramatic and fun, no matter what the subject, are going to win your vote every time. Especially if they include you in the "script" and allow you to show everyone how clever you are.

SUBJECTS

You're a performer, Leo, so you love drama and improvisation. Business studies should give you some background if you want to be mega-rich (if?), and music and painting should both excite your creativity. Sports are great for letting off steam (as long as you're in charge), but you might not be

too enthusiastic about woodworking or science—too fiddly and no glamour. You won't even enjoy drama much if they ask you to work backstage.

HOMEWORK
If a friend suggests going out for some fun just as you're settling down to some algebra, you'll be horribly tempted to add x and y and come up with an hour at the ice rink. Once you remember that you might look bad if you don't get good marks, you'll usually pile up the books and work till you've got it all done. You'll want to be proud of what it looks like, so you'll do your best to make sure it's well presented.

67

STUDYING AND EXAMS

This is where your limitless optimism really takes over. If you're sure you'll pass it'll inspire your performance on the day but it might keep you from studying until the last minute. Give yourself more time and you'll really shine.

In exams you might find that the questions you were so sure would come up haven't. It's that limitless optimism again. If you've studied thoroughly you'll sail through and beam on your way out.

VIRGO

IN THE CLASSROOM

It's not important for you to stand out as a big cheese in the class, Virgo. You'd much prefer to work away quietly, get things done, and do them *perfectly*! You might not like the way your history teacher forgets to dot her "i's," and you've probably got several words to say about the way they dress in the English department, but that won't stop you from doing your best in their lessons.

Being told what to do doesn't usually bother you at all. In fact you rather enjoy being given a definite plan to follow. If you're made to take part in role playing though, or asked to do a five-minute talk on your nicest-ever pet, you might well want to dive under the desk till the bell rings. It'd be a shame if you did because the class would miss out on some good jokes and brilliant observations.

The next time you're feeling shy and reserved, why not imagine yourself being rooted and strong, like a tree in the earth. By the time your roots have gone down so far that they've encouraged your branches to meet the ceiling, you should be confident enough to talk for half an hour.

You just hate being unprepared, so a teacher who makes snap decisions and catches you off guard might make you anxious. Apart from that, you're so easy to teach that you probably get along well with everyone.

SUBJECTS

Being put in the spotlight unnerves you a bit, so drama might not be a hot favorite. Team sports are a bit noisy and out of control so aerobics might be more fun. All the sciences are very appealing. Graphics, design, and cooking are interesting. English is essential to your writing skills. You should love textiles, woodwork, or any subject that allows you to use your hands to make intricate things.

Nadia Listens to Her Inner Critics

HOMEWORK

Once you've gotten the papers into shape, put new batteries in your calculator, sharpened pencils, lined up erasers, arranged pens in sections according to color, and put all reference books in alphabetical order, it'll be bedtime. When you actually get down to it, you'll work effortlessly, neatly, and productively. You'll probably enjoy it as well.

STUDYING AND EXAMS
Studying is easy, except that you might be worrying about the exams so much that you're chewing your pens down faster than you can write up your notes.

Once you're in the exam you'll be completely prepared, cool, and efficient, so don't doubt yourself for a minute. Why not take three extra subjects for good luck?

LIBRA

IN THE CLASSROOM
Just like the scales that symbolize your sign, Libra, you're always struggling to find a perfect point of balance. Your extremes can be so great that you might sometimes feel like you're going up and down on a seesaw.

You'll work so hard for a few days that you astound everyone, including yourself. Then you'll stop completely and lie around till you pick up steam again. This will clearly confuse your teachers, who might be faced with a whirring dynamo at the start of the week and a dozy heap by the end of it.

Being *told* what to do doesn't exactly send you into raptures. You're surprisingly stubborn for one so charming and can dig your heels in (very sweetly) when pushed. If you understand the point of what you're being asked to do and you're in one of your "up" swings, then of course you'll do it perfectly. If you're rattled because you think you've been asked to do something unreasonable, imagine a pendulum swinging wildly from side to side. Let it slowly settle and stop. When the pendulum's still you should feel soothed enough to get on with your work and smile!

SUBJECTS

The arts are number one favorites: drawing, painting, music, dance, and design. With your gift for communication you should enjoy English, drama, foreign languages, and any form of debate. The subjects you don't really like are detail-oriented, so don't feel too hopeless if you shy away from engineering and cutting up amphibians.

HOMEWORK

Once you start you shouldn't have any problems at all. Having decided, that *now* is the moment, you then have to go through the rigmarole of deciding which subject to do first. Toss a coin?

Your work's got to look beautiful too, so you might spend some time adding illustrations or just using color to brighten things up.

STUDYING AND EXAMS

Choosing which subjects to take might present a dilemma. Once you've decided, then it's just that It-Can-Wait-Till-Tomorrow factor that you have to watch out for. Paint a poster that says "Never put off till tomorrow what you can put off till the day after" and throw darts at it.

Once you're in an exam, don't spend too long deciding which question to answer. Then let your cool, clear, clever mind take over—and relax.

SCORPIO

IN THE CLASSROOM

Only one person can actually be in control as far as you're concerned, Scorpio. You.

If you're not interested in what a teacher has to say, you'll go willfully deaf. If you don't want to work you won't pick up a pen, but if you devote your heart and soul to a teacher who's inspired you, a pack of howling wolves won't put you off.

So how will you react if you're told what to do? It all depends on who's telling you. That inspiring teacher's only got to whisper it once and—whoosh—it'll be done.

If another teacher's making you feel mutinous, the whole situation could get rather heated. You can get fairly atomic when you really dig your heels in, and if you meet an equally determined teacher—BOOM!

Apart from the Scorpion, the other creature that's connected to Scorpio is the magnificent, keen-eyed Eagle. If you're locked in a drama, why not imagine that you're spreading those enormous wings and flying away to a very high tree. Once you're really above the situation you might feel calm enough to see the teacher's point of view and get on with whatever you've been asked to do. Well, you *might*...

SUBJECTS
You can do absolutely anything well if you want to. With your piercing mind you'll love all the sciences, from human biology to engineering and psychology. English, music, and painting all feed your imagination and let you express some of those deep, secret feelings in a creative way. Sports are great—because you can develop super-human control and defeat opponents just by *looking* at them. History is full of powerful people you can use as role models.

HOMEWORK
Whatever you do, you always do whole heartedly. If you're deep into the breeding habits of the Tufted Duck then the rest of your life will be put on hold as you research long into the night. If you don't feel like doing something, remember the potential explosion and think about that Eagle. As you hate anything sloppy, you'll do your best to make your work look good and easy to read.

STUDYING AND EXAMS
You'd probably like to look back at whatever exam papers you can get hold of and set yourself up a campaign plan. Once you're sure you understand the system, you'll be in control—your favorite place! During the exams you'll be super-cool and brilliant, and might even enjoy them.

SAGITTARIUS

IN THE CLASSROOM
Who's that wagging a relentless finger and giving an illustrated lecture on The Point Of It All? Is it a department head? Is it your tutor? No—it's YOU!

You're a great fan of fair play, Sagittarius, and you really believe in equal opportunities for all. The problem is that you think you know more than anyone else about being equal and fair (and everything else besides). Any teacher who's trying to exert a little authority over the class may well have to cope with you being affronted at the very idea before work can start at all.

Because you're so good natured and exuberant, particularly when you're really enthusiastic about a teacher or a subject, no one can stay mad at you for long. You want to understand what's being said, instead of learning it parrot fashion, and in trying to understand, you might sometimes get impatient and a bit long-winded yourself.

The Sagittarian centaur is half human and half horse, so why not imagine that your horse is stampeding away and you're going to rein it in, gently and surely. As it clatters to a halt, you can slow down yourself and sit quietly till you get your breath back.

SUBJECTS
With your hunger for travel, geography has to be a special favorite—just drool over those magical place names and wish. All sports are marvelous for your "horse" and you should relish sociology, history, politics, and languages.

Drama gets you entertaining the school and religious education helps you work out your personal philosophy. Making small wooden boxes, cooking, and using water colors could drive you completely up the wall.

HOMEWORK

If that horse in you is really desperate for a good gallop it'll never let you settle down to work, so check out which bit of you is calling loudest before you start. You'll work really well when you're relaxed.

Presentation isn't your best feature. Actually it's your worst and probably loses you marks. Your style's too BIG to be cramped by silly little things like legible handwriting, paragraphs, and punctuation.

STUDYING AND EXAMS

As intelligent as you are, you do sometimes rely on good luck to see you through and that's your biggest problem when it comes to studying. Luck's usually sitting in your pocket waiting to leap out and give you a nice surprise, but it always works better if you feed it with plenty of effort. During exams you should be feeling optimistic and confident, but please practice being tidy, go easy on the jokes, and remember to leave yourself enough time to check over what you've written.

CAPRICORN

IN THE CLASSROOM

You're actually rather keen on rules, Capricorn. A uniformed, organized, disciplined school helps you to feel secure. When you're secure you'll work even harder.

You don't usually mind being told what to do because you can see the value of authority and look forward to having plenty yourself.

You're much more anxious about being taken seriously and can't stand it when you feel ridiculed or even underestimated. You'd like to be treated as an equal and have probably felt like that since you were very tiny (and having business meetings about when to change your diaper).

If a teacher makes fun of you, however affectionately, or you're all chewed up because your dignity's been bruised, what can you do to feel adequate and successful again?

You could think of that Capricorn goat and imagine yourself climbing a really craggy, awkward mountain. You're so sure-footed that it won't take you long to reach the top. Then you can look down on your problems and feel strong and capable again.

SUBJECTS
You're interested in everything to do with the past, so history's likely to be a special favorite. You'll know exactly where you are with math, business, and all the sciences. Your creative side should bloom with ceramics, drawing, and woodworking. Music melts your heart, and English is your foundation for success.

Being in the spotlight usually feels a bit nerve-racking, so having to stand up and do anything in front of the class (or even worse, the school) might make those Capricorn knees knock quite loudly.

HOMEWORK
You could do your homework in a shopping center or on a camping table with a full choir singing carols in your left ear. Your concentration's remarkable and your presentation's excellent. You'll work patiently and extremely hard. The only help you need is a reminder to STOP and have some fun every few weeks or so.

STUDYING AND EXAMS
Studying is not a problem either, except that you might worry too much and that'll start to chip away at your confidence. You're probably doing enough studying to get top grades in every subject so remember to look in a mirror, make a funny face, and laugh the next time you start to doubt yourself. In exams, you'll have no trouble organizing your time or choosing which questions to answer. Take a deep breath when you turn the paper over and think of it as the easiest mountain you've ever climbed.

AQUARIUS

IN THE CLASSROOM
Once you've made your mind up, Aquarius, it would be just as well not to confuse you with the facts. You've got an unshakeable belief in your own ideas, and because they're

often quite progressive and unusual, you might have some wicked battles when you come up against traditional systems.

You're brilliant at devising solutions to apparently insoluble problems, which is great for your own work but just as valuable to the class when a project's falling apart. You'll tie a rubber band to the camshaft, change aerials, paint it pink, and BINGO! Believe in those flashes of inspiration—you might even find they work while you're asleep, so you wake up knowing what to do and how to do it.

When you're faced with authority of any kind, your natural inclination is to rebel, even if you're not sure what you're rebelling about. If a teacher tells you to do something, you could easily turn into a huge cactus and refuse to cooperate. This could lead to life-long ignorance about the Amazon Basin and empirical probability, so why not imagine that your cactus is disappearing and that you're turning into a huge, empty jug that's longing to be filled with all kinds of information. You can always empty it into your homework.

SUBJECTS

Computer studies suit your clever, inventive mind, as do electronics, technology of all kinds, and any of the sciences. You'll be fascinated by psychology, sociology, and the politics of history and geography. English is essential to you. Music's good—particularly if it's electronic. And as you don't like being stuck indoors for too long, sports should blow away all the cobwebs.

You'll enjoy almost anything if the work doesn't get too monotonous but you're more comfortable with subjects you can deal with logically.

HOMEWORK

You're quick and bright and full of enthusiasm, so if you can tear yourself away from the dozens of other things that are spread around your room, you'll get along fine. Unless you've lost your books somewhere in the muddle, in which case you might get distracted while you're looking for them and have to get up at dawn to finish up. Presentation might be a bit untidy, partly because you'll have trodden on it a few times while you were looking for something else.

STUDYING AND EXAMS
You'll work hard and breeze through your studying. During exams you'll need to remember that the answers you've decided on may not entirely suit the questions you've been given. You'll hopefully know so much by then that you'll be able to adapt and survive.

PISCES
IN THE CLASSROOM
You're a great dreamer, Pisces, and the scramble of the school day doesn't leave many spaces for staring out the window at passing clouds. You'll drift off anyway and sit quietly in your corner while facts slip in through one ear, swim about a bit, and float gently out the other.

Being told what to do can sometimes feel like a huge relief, particularly if you're staring at a blank page and you haven't got a clue how to fill it. Your worst reaction might be to complain in a grumbly sort of way, but you'll get through it all right enough because you hate unpleasant atmospheres and angry teachers.

When you're really involved in a lesson, or with a particular teacher or subject, you'll be as receptive as the blackboard is to chalk. If you're bored and everything's gray and dismal you won't feel like learning anything.

You could imagine that you're sitting in a cold puddle when a ladder comes down out of the sky and lands beside you. As you climb out of the puddle and up the ladder the sky becomes dazzling and full of stars. Try getting back to the lesson now. You should be feeling a lot less soggy.

SUBJECTS
You're a natural poet so the creative writing in English should be fun. You can't do without drawing, painting, music, dance, and drama, which doesn't leave much time to spare. History's full of exciting stories, and religious education lets you think about life beyond the material plane.

Ball games are potentially unpleasant, but swimming's fun—you're a fish! Subjects with little or no romance won't be attractive to you so you might not get overexcited about geography, math, or engineering.

HOMEWORK
Homework can be a bit of a chore at times and you've made a serious hobby of dodging things you don't enjoy. Do the most difficult work first and very soon after you get home. A few minutes delay can escalate into a major seize-up if you don't act quickly. Turn off any distractions, shut the door, and jot down a timetable for the work you've got to do. By the time you've finished you'll still have time to yourself (and you'll only feel guilty if you hide in the closet and waste all that talent). Being neat and tidy doesn't come easily to you, but you'll want things to look nice so you'll try.

STUDYING AND EXAMS
Make that timetable much bigger so that it stretches over the weeks you'll need for revision. Why not make the timetable a work of art just to get you in the mood? Remember to double-check which exam you're going to—a calculator won't help you much in still life drawing. When you're actually there in front of the paper, keep an eye on the clock and let all those lovely intuitive answers come tumbling out.

5. ...AND THEN?

Your Sun sign won't entirely describe the kind of career you're interested in but there's bound to be a link of some kind between them.

Sometimes it's a very obvious connection: caring Cancerian, Dr. Barnardo, set up a series of homes for needy children; inventive Aquarian Thomas Edison conceived the lightbulb and the gramophone; and regal Leo has at least three striking examples in England's royal family—Princess Margaret, Princess Anne, and the Queen Mother!

Sometimes the link isn't obvious at all. How could Capricorn, the cautious, ambitious builder, possibly describe Dolly Parton? And how could family-centered, super-sensitive Cancer describe Nelson Mandela?

Dolly Parton comes from a very poor background and has worked hard to become a highly successful songwriter, singer, and actress. She has the Moon in theatrical Leo to account for her star quality, but she's also a brilliant business woman and knows exactly how to capitalize on her talents, thanks to her Capricorn sun.

Nelson Mandela's family could almost be described as the black population of South Africa. He has Mars in Libra to describe his skills as a peace-seeking negotiator and Mercury in Leo to suggest his gifts as an orator, but it's that Cancerian need to care for people and make them safe that seems to have motivated him throughout his long years of struggle.

When it comes to finding an appropriate career, the elements are a useful way of describing the basic needs of each sign:

Fire (Aries, Leo, Sagittarius) looks for adventure and purpose
Earth (Taurus, Virgo, Capricorn) has to be practical
Air (Gemini, Libra, Aquarius) wants to communicate ideas
Water (Cancer, Scorpio, Pisces) needs to involve the emotions

The actual careers associated with your Sun sign may not make you yell, "That's IT!," but there will always be a quality you can bring from your Sun sign to whatever job you choose.

ARIES

ESSENTIALS
Look for a job that allows you a certain amount of independent action—even if it's within a company framework. The more challenges you have to face, the more you'll enjoy yourself, and if you can dash about and shout a lot you'll be ecstatic. Money's important to you but not nearly as important as adventure, so no well-paid, tedious job is going to fulfill you in the end.

POSSIBLE JOBS
Being a firefighter is dangerous and challenging, and you'd get to wear a hat (you rather like uniforms). Driving an ambulance and being a paramedic would involve plenty of speed and activity. You could equally enjoy teaching P.E., working in a sports center, or even taking up a sport professionally.

You'd be a good project leader with young people, a dynamic politician, and an excellent engineer or mechanic.

Why not think about training for a career that would allow you to be self-employed?

FAMOUS ARIES PEOPLE
Eddie Murphy   — actor
Diana Ross   — singer
Maya Angelou   — novelist and poet

Warren Beatty	— actor/producer
Emma Thompson	— actress
Reba McEntire	— singer

TAURUS

ESSENTIALS

You need a job that offers you quite a stable, set routine—even if it's self-imposed. Responsibility won't bother you at all and you'll feel really good if you've got something physical to show for all your hard work.

Aim to earn a substantial amount so that you can buy all those essential (to you) luxuries and have some left over to save. Having plenty of money's vital to your sense of well-being, so you'll always look for ways of insuring a decent income.

POSSIBLE JOBS

Because you're so productive, you'd make a natural farmer, a green-thumbed gardener, and a creative florist. You could build houses or build up businesses. By working as a stockbroker or accountant, you could advise other people on how to make their money double in value.

If you decide to go into the arts you'll sing beautifully, dance divinely, and make sensuous pottery and sculpture. You'd enjoy the retail trade too, especially if you're selling gorgeous, expensive things.

FAMOUS TAURUS PEOPLE

Janet Jackson	— singer/songwriter
André Agassi	— tennis player
Florence Nightingale	— the founder of modern nursing
Michelle Pfeiffer	— actress
Shakespeare	— playwright
"Sugar" Ray Robinson	— boxer

GEMINI

ESSENTIALS

Your dream job would offer you a very varied timetable. You need to get out and meet people, learn new skills as you're going along, and change your routine every day. You'll be happy to take responsibility for yourself but you won't enjoy working alone for long, so don't opt for an isolated office or you'll be talking to your pen.

You're a bit haphazard with money, and it'll never be a priority for you. Finding work that's really stimulating is far more important.

POSSIBLE JOBS

Interpreting for the European parliament, working in public relations, driving a taxi, or being a receptionist in a busy office would all keep you happily on your toes.

You'd make a good teacher, an excellent copywriter in an advertising agency, a funny stand-up comic, and an interesting journalist.

Publishing, computer programming, or graphic design all suit you perfectly. And if you want to talk to millions of people you could always be a weather forecaster, a news anchor, or a soap star.

FAMOUS GEMINI PEOPLE

Marilyn Monroe — actress
Steffi Graf — tennis player
Prince — musician/songwriter/singer/producer
John F. Kennedy — former President of the United States
Candice Bergen — actress
Walt Whitman — poet

CANCER

ESSENTIALS

Whatever job you decide on, you'll need to feel happy

about the atmosphere you're working in and sure that what you're doing is worthwhile.

If you feel safe, you'll be quite set on staying put, taking responsibility and making a name for yourself within the "family" of your company or organization.

Money matters very much and a nice big bank account will make you feel warm all over. You won't have any trouble saving. You're more likely to have trouble remembering where you've hidden your checkbook.

POSSIBLE JOBS

With your love of children, you'd make a caring preschool teacher, nursery nurse, or swimming coach. You'd be a considerate doctor or hospital nurse too, with patients big or small. Catering or hotel management would give you the chance to feed crowds of people, and if you were a real estate agent or property developer you could house them.

You'd be a good politician, too, but if the artist in you comes first, why not try interior decorating, fashion design, or painting?

FAMOUS CANCER PEOPLE

Harrison Ford — actor
Princess Diana — princess
Tom Cruise — actor
Georgio Armani — fashion designer
Bill Cosby — actor/producer
Janice Merrill — track athlete

LEO

ESSENTIALS

With your gifts as an organizer and your natural sense of leadership, you're ideally suited to being boss. The more authority you're given, the more delighted you'll be—particularly when you can get other people to take care of the boring bits while you create the vision.

As long as you're never taken for granted, you'll be happy to stay in one place and build on your success.

Money's essential to you. You just hate to be the old meanie in the corner who can't afford to splurge on treats so you'll make sure that you've got an abundant income.

POSSIBLE JOBS
Being a teacher would suit you perfectly—you could inspire people and inject real drama into your subject.

Acting's the most obvious career for you but you could direct or produce equally well and you'd make a theatrical event out of any sport you took up professionally.

You could build up a business empire, take up modeling, or make a million in the jewelry trade.

FAMOUS LEO PEOPLE
Neil Armstrong   — astronaut
Bill Clinton   — President of the United States
Madonna   — singer/actress
Napoleon   — emperor and military leader
Pete Sampras   — tennis player
Robert De Niro   — actor

VIRGO

ESSENTIALS
Work's vital to your well-being, and you'll even find things to do on your day off. Routine relaxes you. You'd much rather slave away in the background than see your name in lights.

You're not likely to look for a dominant role, but you will need a job that's steady, mentally invigorating, and lets you make full use of your keen eye and steady hand.

You're quite prudent with money but it won't motivate you—even if you found a goose that laid golden eggs you'd want to carry on working.

POSSIBLE JOBS

You could scrutinize anything and find the one dropped stitch or missing comma, so editor, critic, and inspector (of absolutely everything) would all suit you perfectly.

You'd be a good dietitian, an accurate pharmacist, a gentle vet, a perceptive counselor, and a superb doctor or nurse. (You could sterilize everything).

Accounting and statistics would please your love of figures. Your creative side could design jewelry, make beautiful furniture, or write a best-seller.

FAMOUS VIRGO PEOPLE

Mother Theresa   — famous for her charity work in India
Macauley Culkin — actor
Keanu Reeves   — actor
Agatha Christie — author
Roald Dahl   — author
Michael Jackson — singer/songwriter

LIBRA

ESSENTIALS

The people you're working with are just as important as the job you're doing, so look for a nice atmosphere and attractive working conditions.

Rather than being the Big Boss, you'd much prefer to share responsibility and decision making with a partner or a team. You'll need money to fill your life with pretty things, but you'd never work with horrible people just to get rich.

POSSIBLE JOBS

Being a personnel officer would give you every chance to put people at ease (and you could smile a lot). Making people look good would please you too, so why not consider being a beautician, makeup artist, hairdresser, or fashion consultant? You could even give their homes a face-lift and be an interior designer.

You'd be a good diplomat, a sensitive arbitrator in industrial disputes, a clever lawyer, or an optimistic employee in a dating agency. And you're a gifted painter and writer too.

FAMOUS LIBRA PEOPLE

Gandhi	—	Indian leader and pacifist
Jim Henson	—	creator of the Muppets
Sting	—	musician/songwriter/actor
Jayne Torvill	—	ice skater

Martina Navratilova — tennis player and writer
Alfred Nobel — inventor of dynamite and founder of the Nobel Peace Prize

SCORPIO

ESSENTIALS

You won't want to spend time doing anything superficial. Look for a job that has a serious underlying purpose where you can really put that analytical mind to work. You take control effortlessly, so you'll eventually need a free hand to organize your own time (and everybody else's!).

Anything shabby or second-hand really offends you so you'll always want enough money to buy the best. But you might slip into your All or Nothing mode and decide to give everything away, live in a hut, and eat berries.

POSSIBLE JOBS

Investigative work of all kinds would appeal to you because you like to get to the bottom of interesting mysteries, so you'd be a probing private eye, an inquiring pathologist, or a gritty detective.

Surgery, psychotherapy, and scientific research would all give you the opportunity to help people in need. You could use all that relentless energy in the arts as a musician, poet, or painter. You might even decide to go to sea!

FAMOUS SCORPIO PEOPLE

Julia Roberts — actress
Hillary Clinton — lawyer and First Lady of the U.S.A.
Prince Charles — heir to the throne of England
Whoopi Goldberg — actress
Madame Curie — awarded Nobel Prize twice for the discoveries of radioactivity and radium
Pablo Picasso — artist

SAGITTARIUS

ESSENTIALS

You need a job that gives you room to grow and learn. The more freedom you have the happier you'll be. Being part of a larger system suits you well, but you're self-motivated and don't really like or need direction to achieve your potential.

You're ridiculously extravagant and money seems to evaporate as soon as it meets your pocket, so no matter how much you earn you'll always wish you could be earning more.

POSSIBLE JOBS

Being a travel agent would give you the chance to talk about exploring. Being an actual explorer might suit you even better. You could be a courier, a travel writer, an interpreter, or an anthropologist so that you can learn about the people you want to visit.

Lecturing or working in academia would let you explore the world intellectually, and you'd be equally happy as a lawyer or professor.

You'd be good with animals (particularly horses), a dynamic sports professional, and an exceptional entertainer.

FAMOUS SAGITTARIUS PEOPLE

Walt Disney — Film animator and producer
Tina Turner — singer
William Blake — visionary/mystic/poet/painter
Joe DiMaggio — baseball player
Jane Austen — author
Steven Spielberg — film producer/director

CAPRICORN

ESSENTIALS

You're ambitious and determined so you need a job that'll give you the chance to be really successful. If you're asked to take responsibility for absolutely everything you'll feel very special. The more hard work you're expected to do, the more you'll love it.

Your budgeting skills are excellent, and you'll usually have an efficient savings plan so you need a good enough income to feel secure. Whatever you buy, you'll want the best so that it'll last and save you money in the end.

POSSIBLE JOBS
With your interest in construction you'd do well as an architect, builder, or surveyor. You could develop your organizational skills in civil service, work within the government as a politician, or go into big business and redesign entire commercial systems to save everyone loads of time and money. You'd be a gifted scientist or archaeologist, a skilled physiotherapist, osteopath, or dentist and an ingenious mathematician.

If you decide to do something creative you'd landscape elegant gardens. You've got a special gift for music.

FAMOUS CAPRICORN PEOPLE
Annie Lennox	—	singer/songwriter
Kevin Costner	—	actor
Joan of Arc	—	soldier and saint
Martin Luther King, Jr.	—	civil rights leader
Denzel Washington	—	actor
Kate Moss	—	model

AQUARIUS

ESSENTIALS
You need a job where you're encouraged to think independently and are valued for your inventive brilliance. Whatever you're doing, you need plenty of freedom to change existing structures. And if you've got lots of physical space to do this in you'll be even happier.

Even though you'd never run from personal responsibility,

working in a group really suits you best.

Money's not the most important thing in your choice of career—in fact you can sometimes be a bit absent-minded about your personal day-to-day business altogether.

POSSIBLE JOBS

As you like being in space so much, why not be a pilot or an astronaut? You could design innovative planes and space-ships, develop new electronic systems, and find some unex-pected uses for the microchip.

You'd be a caring social worker, a good radiographer,

and a powerful political reformer. Producing, directing, or writing for television and radio would let you communicate with the maximum number of people. You'd be a really good studio technician, record producer, or photographer.

FAMOUS AQUARIAN PEOPLE

Oprah Winfrey — talk show host/actress/producer
Charles Dickens — author
Vanna White — TV personality
Germaine Greer — author/feminist
Jane Seymour — actress
Abraham Lincoln — former President of the United States

PISCES

ESSENTIALS

Try and find a job that lets you take things at a gentle tempo—you'll be much happier if you don't have to work fast and stick to a rigid routine.

You might prefer not to be in charge, particularly if you have to make loads of decisions and upset your coworkers.

A career won't appeal to you because the pay's good. You'll be far more interested in how you feel about what you're doing.

POSSIBLE JOBS

You could dance, act, make music, paint, or write lyrical poems, stories, and songs.

Hospitals are full of people who'd love you to be a doctor, nurse, or social worker, and you might want to put everyone to sleep and be an anesthesiologist. With your interest in feet you could be a chiropodist, reflexologist, or shoe designer.

You'd be a kindly vet or veterinary nurse (specializing in fish?). You could also make a successful career in the navy.

FAMOUS PISCES PEOPLE
Bruce Willis	— actor
Albert Einstein	— mathematician
Michelangelo	— painter/sculptor
Glenn Close	— actress
Elizabeth Barrett Browning	— poet
Drew Barrymore	— actress

6. HOME, HOBBIES, VACATIONS, AND HOW YOU LOOK

ARIES

FAMILY MATTERS

You're usually on the move, so however much you care about your family, you won't want to spend much time sitting cozily by the fire.

As you speed independently about, dropping china and banging doors, you do occasionally find time for a few invigorating words with passing relations, but they'd probably appreciate you even more if you'd only slow down a bit.

If you've got any brothers or sisters, they're probably used to you taking the lead and losing your temper every now and again when they're being a bit slow or stubborn. They'll love your energy and sense of fun though, and the way you always stick up for them when they're in trouble.

CHORES

A mighty duster-bearing whirlwind couldn't get around a room as fast as you can. It might get around a bit more often though. Cleaning up isn't really an attractive proposition when there are so many other more important things to do. At least you're speedy and efficient when you finally get down to it.

YOUR ROOM

You're not very tidy—other more important things to do, etc.—but that old whirlwind does occasionally whizz around, and then you have a new room. For a bit.

You need your room to be functional and brightly

painted, not that you'll spend much time in it. Chances are you don't even mind getting out of bed in the morning!

CLOTHES

If you're going to feel really good about yourself, you need to wear smart, chic clothes that let you move easily and look sharp. You'll like spectacular accessories and bright colors but your special color is red.

FOOD

You love food, but you'd sooner eat a quick (delicious) meal than spend hours in the kitchen constructing something ornamental out of parsnips and mayonnaise. It'll definitely do you more good if you take the time to chew it a few times.

HOBBIES

You're happiest being out and about, going to the gym, learning karate, roller-skating, cycling, playing tennis or another other sport (but you play to WIN!). If you go to see a film or a play it'd better be gripping or you might want to leave before the end.

Every now and again you'll get a wild urge to start something creative, but if The Something can't be finished quickly you might well lose interest and leave it lying around for a year or two (and then throw it away). Memo: choose a project you *know* you can complete beautifully because it's fast.

Pets are fun as long as you don't have to clean out cages, do grooming, or remember feeding times. A bouncy dog would be best for playing games—you might not have time to get a grip on the more subtle qualities of goldfish.

VACATIONS
Whether you go with friends or with your family, the more adventurous and physical your vacation, the more fun you'll have. Find a theme park, go camping, lead an expedition, or take a mountain bike into rugged countryside.

TAURUS

FAMILY MATTERS
As long as nothing disturbs your comfort or upsets your routine, you're usually a good-tempered and affectionate person to have around. If you were asked to move into another room, though, or told you had to move altogether, you'd probably want to glue yourself to the floor in an attempt to thwart the inevitable. Flexibility isn't your strong point.

Your family might sometimes think you're being unnecessarily stubborn, but it really is quite difficult for you to adapt to change.

If you've got any brothers or sisters they might not like it when you're being dictatorial or telling them what they can borrow and for how long—if at all! They'll know they can rely on you, though, and they'll love you for your warmth and common sense.

CHORES
Because you so like being comfortable, you're quite good at doing your share of housework (as long as you can relax and enjoy the results). If you're in one of your obstinate phases you might prefer to enjoy the results of someone else's efforts.

YOUR ROOM
Even if your room isn't completely tidy, you'll want it to be welcoming and restful. You need to be comfortable and you'd probably prefer harmonious pastel colors, lots of cushions, and nice things to look at on the walls.

Bouncing out of bed isn't your favorite way to start the day. Why would you want to leave such a lovely, soft, warm place? Perhaps the thought of breakfast might tempt you to lift the covers.

CLOTHES
You're easily spotted in a clothes shop. You'll *feel* what you're buying as well as look at the price, style, and color. If a beautiful jumper feels like an old tow-rope, you won't even bother to try it on. Your clothes should be soft, natural, and easy to wear. Flowery prints, cotton, silk, and linen all look good on you and your special colors are green, pink, and blue.

FOOD
This is a very important part of your life—and rightly so. You've got a special genius for cooking (and eating). If your family is very lucky you've been making them delicious food since you were big enough to grease a cake pan.

HOBBIES
You could always make a serious hobby out of your dancing skills. Whatever kind of dancing you choose you'll have enormous fun and get plenty of exercise while you're enjoying yourself. What about growing something edible? Even if it's herbs on the windowsill, you'll be really proud when you serve them up as "home produce."

You could make lovely clothes or pottery, bake bread and cakes, or make music to your heart's content.

If you've got a pet you'll love stroking and cuddling it, so you'll be a lot happier if it's warm-blooded and got four legs. Steer clear of newts and tarantulas.

VACATIONS
If you can settle into a good vacation routine you'll have a great time. Get up late, go for nice slow walks to absorb nature (followed by nice teas absorbing cake), and find some interesting shops to explore.

GEMINI

FAMILY MATTERS
You love family life if there's plenty of bustle and activity. If you know you're being listened to and understood as well then you won't need much more to be content.

You might make them all a bit dizzy sometimes when you're being a particularly busy Gemini butterfly. Perhaps you could settle in one place long enough to enjoy the flowers and find out what everyone else is up to?

If you've got any brothers or sisters, they'll love the way you're always ready for fun and conversation. They'll hopefully have learned to concentrate on their homework while you're chatting. With any luck they'll still be laughing at your brilliant impersonations of them (and anyone else you all know).

CHORES

It's not that you're unwilling to help out, but your idea of housework is to move a few things about and then add a few more. If you keep everything of yours in your topsy-turvy room at least you'll be the only one who has to look at it.

YOUR ROOM

This is the place where you can really spread out. You need light, bright colors and plenty of shelves, drawers, cupboards, and surfaces to put all your paraphernalia. Sadly, the more space you've got the more you'll find to fill it (Ancient Law). You'll probably want to go to bed quite late and get up quite early. If you share a room, be considerate of the other occupant.

CLOTHES

You'll want to be seen in clothes that are a bit out of the ordinary and easy to look after because you're so busy. Stripes, dots, and small patterns all suit you, and your special colors are pale gray, violet, and pale yellow.

FOOD

The thing you enjoy most about eating is the chance to get together and discuss the day. If you're on your own you'll probably eat when you must and watch television or read at the same time (and ruin all your clothes). Cooking isn't your favorite way of spending time.

HOBBIES

Some of your hobbies might involve words. You could write to a pen pal, keep a diary, start a newspaper, or fill a scrapbook. If you're in the mood for sports you'll be good at fencing, tennis, badminton, and squash. Computer games, card tricks, and charades would all use your agile brain and fingers, and you'd probably enjoy puzzles and mathematical brainteasers. When it comes to pets you'd enjoy having a bird that you could teach to answer back, and a clever dog would be a really good friend (you'd have fun training it from the puppy stage).

VACATIONS
Activity vacations suit you much better than the sort where you lie about and doze. Long walks, camping, sight-seeing, skiing, or windsurfing would all give you a really good rest. You'll enjoy everything more if you're with people you can talk to and you might even decide to take an educational break so that you can learn something new while you're having a vacation.

CANCER
FAMILY MATTERS
You're such a family-centered person that you'll usually enjoy being at home more than anything else. Taking care of things comes easily to you and you'll often be the first to make sure that everyone's all right. It might take a while for your family to really understand how shy and sensitive you can be. Don't be too quick to rush off in a huff if somebody doesn't appreciate your feelings right away.

If you've got any brothers or sisters they'll know they can always rely on your kindness when they're scared or down in the dumps. They'll have learned to disappear when you're feeling crabby and to give you giant hugs when you're feeling calm again.

CHORES
As you enjoy being at home so much you won't usually mind lending a hand to clean it up. In fact you're a bit of a wizard at making a room look pretty and tidy and having a good time while you're doing it.

YOUR ROOM
Here's where you can snuggle under the blanket and feel

safe. It's *very difficult* for you to get up.

Unless you're having a moody day it'll look cozy and neat and feel very comfortable. (Moody days are usually spent in a small shell with no proper view of the outside world, including domestic chaos.) You need soft, gentle colors and plenty of room for all the things you can't bear to throw away in case they come in handy.

CLOTHES

You like soft clothes that are comfortable but smart. Natural fibers and subtle colors suit you best and you are quite restrained in the way you add jewelry or accessories. Your special colors are white, cream, and pale green.

FOOD

Cooking and eating are special pleasures for you, and you love presenting your family with all the scrumptious goodies you've created. You'd always prefer to get everyone together around the table—wolfing down sandwiches isn't your idea of a proper meal at all.

HOBBIES

You'll enjoy doing quite a lot in your room. You can read, paint, sew, listen to music, or spend hours looking at all the fascinating things you've collected.

Swimming's good exercise and you'll probably get a lot out of aquarobics or dancing (on dry land).

You love animals and the more affectionate they are the better. Dogs are a particular favorite but you'll happily care for any creature you come into contact with. Well, almost.

VACATIONS

Going on vacation isn't usually as appealing as the thought of staying at home, especially if you have to leave your pets behind. If you do go away you'll probably have a great time, so don't get too jittery when you're packing. A family

cottage or villa by the sea would be perfect. You could turn your bit of it into a home-away-from-home and really relax. You might even enjoy being on a ship, as long as you've got somewhere comfortable to sleep and plenty of good food.

LEO

FAMILY MATTERS

When you feel important and special, you're a sunny, affectionate, and generous person to live with. You can try out all your creative ideas on your family and order them around (if they'll let you). There might be times when they won't want to do things quite the way you'd planned—

perhaps you'll be generous enough to let them have their way for a while?

If you've got any brothers or sisters they'll have learned just how forceful and determined you can be, especially if you rope them into your schemes and give them all supporting roles. They'll love your laughter and enthusiasm and they'll know they can rely on your loyalty no matter what.

CHORES
You like to see everything looking tidy and clean, but you'd much sooner delegate the actual work to someone else than pick up a duster or vacuum the floor yourself. If you ever feel humble enough to try, you'll clean things beautifully and need masses of praise afterwards for your superhuman efforts.

YOUR ROOM
You'll need your room to be a light, brightly painted operations base for all your projects. Make sure you've got a nice, big mirror to act in front of and an area for planning whatever new venture's on the go. You're quite tidy at heart but read "Chores" again and remember that even people who enjoy housework need time off. You could always try doing it yourself.

You can sleep on and on and on, until you're hungry enough to get up.

CLOTHES
You want to be noticed and admired, so you wear dramatic, image-conscious clothes with distinctive extras and plenty of glitter! You'll make any fabric or color look good, but your special colors are yellow and gold.

FOOD
A piece of toast on a cracked plate isn't going to please you as much as steaming pancakes on a golden dish. If you don't want to go to quite those lengths you can still make ordin-

ary meals special by the way you serve things. You love eating and enjoy cooking, but when it comes to cleaning up, uh-oh.

HOBBIES
Performing (what else!) has to be top of the list. You'll be in your element if you join a drama group, play in a band, or find some other way to take to the stage.

Games of all kinds give you the chance to be exuberant, but you'll really love any sport that allows you to make an entrance, do something splendid, and exit to loud cheers and thunderous applause.

Although you'll always have fun playing with dogs, you're likely to have a special place in your heart for cats— you're one of the big cats after all.

VACATIONS
If you're really going to have a good time you need plenty of lovely weather so you can laze around like a lion. You'd relish a luxury hotel or a cruise, but any vacation that lets you relax all day and then have fun in the evening is going to leave you purring.

VIRGO

FAMILY MATTERS
You're quite a private person, but you still want to be part of the family. As long as you can spend some time by yourself doing the things that interest you, you'll be happy to join in with family activities, too.

As you walk about putting things away, picking up bits of fluff, checking surfaces for dust, and correcting any mistakes your family might be making about the news, the neighbors, the next world, don't forget that they might *enjoy* not being perfect every now and again.

If you've got any brothers or sisters they will have had to learn to leave you in peace when you want to be quiet and think, and *never* to disorganize your room. When you're in the mood to talk they'll love your common sense advice and the sweet way you always help them to see the funny side of any problem while you're busy solving it.

CHORES
You do them quite often and rather well.

YOUR ROOM
On the rare days when your room's a bit messy you'll still be able to find *exactly* what you're looking for because of the filing system you carry in your head. You need an adaptable, tasteful room with plenty of bookshelves, a table for work, and a good source of light to help you do fiddly things more easily.

Getting up rather depends on how busy you were the night before. Even Virgos need to sleep.

CLOTHES
You'll feel chic and elegant in well-cut, understated clothes. (Gold lamé's unlikely, egg stains are out of the question.) Subtle shades suit you best and your special colors are gentle browns, blues, and grays.

FOOD
Eating isn't just a pleasure for you. You'll think about what's gone into the meal, check out your dietary needs (and everyone else's) and cook appetizing things in the most efficient, capable way. You can be quite picky about certain foods and you'd always prefer a few tasty forkfuls to a great steaming heap that obliterates the plate.

HOBBIES
You've got very clever fingers and you can use them to knit, sew, do embroidery, make jewelry, and carve or paint wood.

You've got a clever mind too, so treat it to chess, mental

puzzles, computer games, and lots of reading.

If you want to exercise, you'd probably prefer walking, swimming, or tennis to anything rugged and noisy.

When it comes to pets, you're a complete pushover. Small furry animals are bewitching, and medium-sized furry animals are irresistible. There may be days when you'd sooner be with your pets than with your friends.

VACATIONS
A working vacation of some kind would actually feel like a rest. You could help out on a farm or take a field trip to learn about nature. You might like to get fit with a week at a health spa or do some really interesting sight-seeing in museums and galleries.

LIBRA

FAMILY MATTERS
You want everyone in your family to be friends—fair play and equal shares for all—so you'll go out of your way to smooth things over if there's a hiccup. They might get a bit exasperated when you're delaying an important decision, so let them know you'll have an answer soon.

If you've got any brothers or sisters they'll have learned not to waste time trying to have petty arguments with you, but they'll love you for your sense of justice and your kind, reasonable nature. And the way you share your sweets.

CHORES
Ugh! Doing these is absolutely not your idea of a well-spent morning. You'll do them to keep the peace but it might help you to think of housework as the first step to a more attractive home. Then again, that might not help at all. Sometimes you just have to grit your teeth and see it as one of life's more infuriating necessities.

YOUR ROOM

You want your room to look nice but you're not exactly wild about cleaning up. So? You shove everything into closets and under the bed, puff up the pillows, spray a bit of polish in the air, and hope to goodness that nobody looks behind the scenery at the horrible truth.

As for getting up—it really depends on your state of mind. You'll either be dressed and ready before the alarm goes off or fast asleep when everyone else has finished breakfast and gone.

CLOTHES

Clothes are a good way for you to practice your design skills and you'll probably have quite a stock of things to wear. You want to look casually elegant and you'll be quite inventive in the way you mix bits and pieces to create a "look." Although your special colors are pink and blue you'll often enjoy wearing black and white together.

FOOD

If you're going to enjoy what you're eating, the atmosphere needs to be calm and relaxed so don't eat in a rush, or worse, in a bad mood.

You like food to be as attractive to the eye as to the stomach, so you'll never throw it haphazardly on the plate. You're more likely to spend ages cutting flowers out of orange peel and weaving parsley around hard-boiled eggs.

HOBBIES

Whatever you're doing, you'll enjoy it more if you're doing it with other people—going to aerobics, the gym, ice-skating, dance classes, making clothes, playing tennis, or just sitting about and chatting. You'll probably have fun making birthday cards for your family and friends, designing clothes, and experimenting with dyes and paints.

You love animals, and if you're going to choose a pet

you'll probably go for a gorgeous creature that's irresistibly sweet and endearing. Don't forget to feed it on your lazy days!

VACATIONS
Go somewhere lovely and explore the beauty spots and works of art, or be artistic yourself and try a painting or drawing week in idyllic surroundings. If you're really going to unwind you'll want to share your fun with a friend or two.

SCORPIO

FAMILY MATTERS
It's not in your nature to take anything lightly and family life's no exception. You expect a lot from people and you give every bit as much in exchange, but you can sometimes carry on alarmingly, particularly if you're feeling thwarted or jealous. Not everyone feels things as deeply as you do, so it might help if you try to explain what the problem is.

If you've got any brothers or sisters, they'll have found out by now that certain areas in your room are *out of bounds,* and they may have discovered (even if they're half-asleep) that you're not that easy to boss around. They'll love you for your fierce loyalty, though, and the way you keep their secrets.

CHORES
Whatever you do, you do properly and if you clean up there won't be a speck of dust or a microbe left—IF you clean up. You might decide to dig your heels in and refuse, but you could just as well take over and do it all.

YOUR ROOM
The most important thing your room can offer you is privacy. You'd probably like a locked box to put special, secret things in and a diary you can lock and put in the box. You

probably keep everything quite tidy. You might want to add a few dramatic touches like screens or draped fabric to make intriguing corners.

Getting up in the morning shouldn't be too difficult, particularly if you're deeply involved in something you can't wait to get back to.

CLOTHES
You like to look snazzy and bewitching, so you'll feel good wearing sophisticated colors and fabrics that emphasize your shape. Wearing anything secondhand won't appeal to you at all. You keep the things you've got in really good condition. Your special colors are dark red and black.

FOOD
The analytical chemist that lives somewhere in your personality is quite likely to approach suspicious-looking food with a microscope. Once you've decided that you like the look and taste of something, you'll eat it day in and day out. If it fails the test then no clever disguises are going to persuade you to change your mind. You can cook well and if you're choosing the ingredients you can be as scrupulous as you like.

HOBBIES
When you're in your room you get a lot of pleasure from music, especially if you're playing an instrument yourself. Reading and writing are good ways of exploring your imagination and you might want to paint, draw, etch, or engrave. When it's time to exercise then swimming and water sports should be fun, and squash or tennis should help you let off steam.

You'll get really closely involved with whatever pet you keep. You could keep exotic tropical fish or even train a falcon!

VACATIONS

A vacation near water would be a good rest for you. You could help to crew a yacht, go canoeing or scuba diving, take long walks by the sea, or look for frozen water and go skiing. If you want your curiosity excited you'd relish a trip to somewhere mysterious like the Pyramids.

SAGITTARIUS

FAMILY MATTERS

Even though you're a born traveler, you love having a family to come home to and share your experiences with. Even if the journey's only been to school and back there might still be some important things to talk about and learn from. Sometimes you might get really excited because you're sure you've got the only sensible solutions to the world's problems. How about negotiating a truce and listening to what the rest of the family has to say? (You probably won't change your mind, but at least you'll have shown a willingness.)

If you've got any brothers or sisters they'll have gotten used to your impatience and decided whether to agree with you or risk an argument. They'll love your optimistic, affectionate good humor and your awful jokes.

CHORES

You'd probably sooner take a hang glider over the Pyrenees in the dark than wash the kitchen floor, so you'll have to find yourself a system if you're not going to be branded as The Person Everyone Has To Clean Up After. You could pretend it's a training session and time yourself, or dress up in silly clothes and imagine it's a film set, or just do it as quickly as possible to avoid being shouted at.

YOUR ROOM

Being neat isn't just at the bottom of your list of priorities—it's *underneath* it. You'll want quite a big room. Paint it brightly to distract you from the clutter and shut the door

to protect the family.

Getting up won't usually bother you but you're not likely to win any medals for punctuality.

CLOTHES
Stiff, tailored styles won't give you the freedom of movement you need at all. You'd prefer casual, comfortable clothes that you can "dress up" when you need to look extra smart. Your special color's purple.

FOOD
Even though you love food you haven't really got the patience to scrub a potato or boil rice. You'd probably prefer

to eat while you're traveling or talking or sitting in a busy restaurant with people to observe and talk about later.

HOBBIES
Reading biographies, books about travel, or adventure stories are bound to whet your appetite for experience and you'll make the most of any chance you get to exercise. Apart from straightforward team games you'd excel at archery, athletics, or cycling. If you wanted to try something with a few risks attached (and you probably do) there's canoeing, climbing, and motocross.

You love animals of all kinds, but you've got a special affinity with horses. If you're going to have a dog you'd prefer it to be big and playful, and you might even get a cat to do entertaining things with string and stuffed woolly mice.

VACATIONS
You could take a bus around America, cycle around Australia, or get on a plane without knowing your destination at all and still have a great time. Whatever vacation you take you'll love the journey, explore the territory when you're there, and feel rotten about having to go back to routine when it's time to leave.

CAPRICORN

FAMILY MATTERS
You're not hugely demonstrative, but you feel very strongly about the family and its traditions and history. You care about everyone in the family circle, no matter how young or old and you really love it when you can all meet up. Sometimes you can be so conscientious that you forget to join in the fun. You could probably abandon your routine once in a while without the sky falling in.

If you've got any brothers or sisters, you'll look after them if they're younger and try to look after them if they're older. They'll know they can't play havoc with your room or disturb your plans but they'll love you for all your care and attention and come to you for help when they're in a mess.

CHORES
Responsibility doesn't usually bother you and you'll probably enjoy setting up a chore list and then doing your share. You could actually do everyone else's share without pausing for breath, but why not stop and listen to the birds singing for a few minutes?

YOUR ROOM
You could really think of your room as your main office. You're neat and efficient, so there won't be any old bits of toast under the bed or abandoned homework stuffed in your hamper.

You'll need places to store things and places to work. When it comes to getting up you're usually the first in the bathroom.

CLOTHES
You're quite traditional so you won't want to upset the neighbors by wearing anything outrageous. You're happier with classic clothes in dark colors that enhance your image, and your special colors are black, dark blue, and dark brown.

FOOD
You're a good cook and you like to keep the kitchen tidy while you're making things. You probably don't enjoy very fussy, complicated food, but you love eating and you'll be even happier if you can get everyone to enjoy a meal together, especially at celebrations and festivals.

HOBBIES
You're a practical person and you get a lot of pleasure out of making things. Model-building, pottery, sculpture, and

carpentry are all good fun and you could even design a little garden—indoor or out.

Reading relaxes you. You might want to collect old coins, dried flowers, or antique toys. You love listening to music or even making your own. If you want some exercise you can go skating, do aerobics, climb, run, or go for long walks.

If you're going to have a pet you'll want it to be quite well-trained and a good companion, so you'll probably enjoy a disciplined dog more than a willful cat!

VACATION
You'll want your vacation to be well-planned. You wouldn't want to wait for a standby ticket or turn up somewhere without a place to sleep. A long excursion in open country with plenty of good food would send you home beaming. You might even enjoy an archaeological dig.

AQUARIUS

FAMILY MATTERS
You want family life to be open and friendly so that everyone can talk and share their ideas and experiences. With your love of space and freedom it won't always be easy for you to cope with some of the restrictions that you're asked to accept. It's just as well. You're rational enough to see the reasons behind the rules.

If you've got any brothers or sisters they'll have found out just how stubborn you can be. They won't expect you to be around all the time, but they'll love your kindness and the way you keep coming up with brilliant ideas.

CHORES
You're so busy wandering off into theories and concepts that you haven't really got time for anything as pointless as cleaning up. Logic tells you it'll only get messy again, so why bother? You might find that the rest of your family

doesn't really appreciate your singular ideas on the science of housework, so you'll just have to find your community spirit and roll up your sleeves.

YOUR ROOM

As you already know, you're not a neat person. You'll want plenty of space (you always do), bright, unusual colors on the walls, and a window you can open wide.

Getting up is dependent on how enthusiastic you are feeling. You can outsleep Rip Van Winkle or be up and out of the house before anyone else is awake.

CLOTHES

You don't want to look like everyone else, no matter how fashion conscious you are. You can wear very conventional clothes (with a difference) or completely eccentric outfits in all kinds of fabric and pattern combinations that could easily stop the traffic. Your special color is electric blue.

FOOD

If you had sole charge of the fridge you'd be lucky to find half a lemon and a stalk of droopy celery. When you do remember to eat you're usually happy to try out all sorts of odd tastes and combinations of ingredients. If you decide to cook something for the family it probably won't look or taste like anything they've ever had before.

HOBBIES

You're a born photographer and you might even want your own darkroom so that you can experiment with developing techniques. Movies, music, reading, and writing are all interesting. You could get involved in astronomy, computer games, or astrology.

You don't like being confined for too long and you should enjoy most team sports, mountain climbing, or cycling. You could even go up in a hot-air balloon or learn to fly a glider!

You're very fond of animals but you won't want a lap-dog or any pet that needs constant attention. Birds or cats would be best (but possibly not at the same time).

VACATIONS
Anywhere, any time, as far away as possible (on a space-ship?). Flying's your favorite means of transport and you probably wish you'd been born a bird from time to time.

If you can't go far away, you'll still enjoy yourself as long as you've got people to meet and places to explore.

PISCES
FAMILY MATTERS
You're always aware of what other people are feeling and that's particularly true of your family. You'll echo the general mood, whether it's happy, disgruntled, or sad and do your very best to help out whenever you can.

Time spent alone is very important to you and your family might not always understand that. Don't just disappear —let them know you'll be back soon!

If you've got any brothers or sisters they'll have learned that you can't be hurried or made to play if you're feeling private, but they'll love you for your gentle kindness and the way you always understand their dreams.

CHORES
The trouble with the castles-in-the-air you live in is that they never seem to need their floors swept. You hate housework. You could always pretend that the chores are a magical task you've been given to break a cruel spell and if you get through them fast enough your favorite pet will turn into a fairy. When it doesn't happen you'll realize you were lying. Next time?

YOUR ROOM

Your room needs to be a place where you can dream and vanish from the world every now and then. Gentle colors and lovely paintings (by you?) help to make it really restful. Neat, isn't it?

You'll need a bed with good springs and a very long guarantee to survive the hours you spend in it.

CLOTHES

You want your clothes to feel soft and look graceful. You might dye boring things to make them more interesting. You could enjoy buying second-hand things from antique shops for a bit of extra glamour. Your special color is sea-green.

FOOD

What a great cook you are! You love making food look beautiful, and you think up great combinations of texture, color, and taste. Eating isn't a problem either—as long as the atmosphere's pleasant and you haven't taken a sudden dislike to whatever it is you were enjoying so much a week ago.

HOBBIES

You love music and you might want to listen, play, or even write some yourself. Dancing gives you the chance to be in a world of your own and use music in a different way.

You could paint or illustrate stories and poems you've written, go to the movies a lot, go swimming, help out on a boat, or go scuba diving.

As far as pets are concerned, you're capable of taking a wheelbarrow out to gather strays. No sick, lost, or needy creature is going to escape your ministrations. You'd better have at least one cat, dog, rabbit, fish, or duck to lavish all that love on.

VACATIONS

A small desert island with a few special people, plenty of delicious food, a comfortable bed, and some lovely music might be all you need to have a perfect holiday. If you can't get to a desert island you'll still need plenty of water—sea, lake, or river—time by yourself, and beautiful things and places to look at.

7. HOW TRUE ARE YOU TO YOUR SUN SIGN?

ARIES

1. It's the school trip. Your teacher suggests some rock-climbing followed by a white-water race in canoes. Do you:
a) get really excited about the activities and join in enthusiastically?
b) join in reluctantly?
c) pretend to have a headache and spend the day lying in bed, eating toast, and watching television?

2. You're in the middle of a terrible argument with a friend. Halfway through the fight you realize all your friend's points are correct and you're completely in the wrong. Do you:
a) gracefully admit your errors?
b) have a coughing fit and go home?
c) carry on regardless?

3. You're helping your little cousin with his homework. After five minutes he still doesn't understand what you're

saying. Do you:
a) get irritable and say you're too busy to help him any more?
b) patiently go over the work again?
c) tempt him to watch a video instead?

4. Your school's organizing a charity marathon and not many people in your class seem to want to get involved. Do you:
a) go along with everyone else and do nothing?
b) tell everyone they've got to do it because it's an important cause?
c) join in so people think you're a nice person?

5. It's the weekend. Do you:
a) create an adventure?
b) plan every little thing you're going to do?
c) get some books from the library and spend the weekend reading in your room?

6. You like your new neighbor. Do you:
a) stare wistfully at her from behind your bedroom curtains?
b) find an excuse to go over and introduce yourself?
c) fall off your bike outside their house and hope to be rescued/noticed?

7. You're on a date with your new boyfriend/girlfriend. Are you:
a) dressed to kill?
b) in the same clothes you've had on all day?
c) wearing the kind of clothes you think your boyfriend/ girlfriend might like?

8. On the same date your boyfriend/girlfriend wants to go to the movies. You've had your mind set on going skating. Do you:

a) smile sweetly and go to the movies?
b) cringe till it's time to go home?
c) go skating?

9. You've just bought some sweets. You're halfway through the package when you find one covered in mold. Do you:
a) throw them out and hope you won't be sick?
b) take the package back to the shop, complain and demand a refund?
c) feel too embarrassed to cause a fuss but avoid the shop in future?

10. If you had to describe yourself as a means of transport would you be:
a) a red sports car?
b) a luxury ocean liner?
c) a golf cart?

1. a) 5   b) 0   c) 0
2. a) 0   b) 0   c) 5
3. a) 5   b) 0   c) 0
4. a) 0   b) 5   c) 0
5. a) 5   b) 0   c) 0
6. a) 0   b) 5   c) 0
7. a) 5   b) 0   c) 0
8. a) 0   b) 0   c) 5
9. a) 0   b) 5   c) 0
10. a) 5   b) 0   c) 0

If you scored:
40–50
You're true to your Sun sign—brave, impatient, inspiring, and pushy.

20–35
You're not *quite* true to your Sun sign. Perhaps you're managing to be dynamic without treading on anyone's toes.

0–15

You don't seem to be as true to your Sun sign as you could be. Suggestions: wear a bright red t-shirt, get plenty of exercise, practice being assertive.

TAURUS

1. A pigeon flies into the classroom. Do you:
a) scream and hide under the desk?
b) open all the windows and wait quietly?
c) run around flapping your arms?

2. You're at a friend's house. It's a cold day and they haven't turned on any heat. Do you:
a) tough it out in a t-shirt?
b) make an excuse, run home and get into a hot bath to warm up?
c) Complain and ask someone to turn the heat on?

3. A friend borrows a book without asking. Would you:
a) pursue him until you get it back?
b) hope he enjoys it?
c) not notice it's missing because you don't really know what books you've got?

4. You love your old bed. You've been told you've got to have a new one:

a) look forward to the change?

b) ask if you can store it somewhere in case it comes in handy one day?

c) resist the change for as long as possible?

5. You go shopping for a new nightgown. Do you:

a) pick something that's scratchy but really fashionable?

b) choose the cheapest one on the sale rack no matter what it looks like?

c) go for the softest, most comfortable gown you can find—even if it's expensive?

6. For the past few months someone in your class has really been getting to you. During this time you've kept calm. Do you eventually:

a) snap?

b) have a quiet sensible chat with your tormentor in the hope that the teasing will stop?

c) ask for a transfer to another class?

7. It's the morning of the summer fair at your school. Everyone is supposed to be there early to help out. Would you:

a) pretend to be ill, not turn up, and feel guilty all day?

b) arrive promptly and help out at the bake sale?

c) arrive late, rush from table to table trying to be helpful, and end up getting in everyone's way?

8. You see your ex at a party with someone new. Do you?

a) feel happy that he/she has found a new romance?

b) go over to them and start chatting about that last wonderful day you had together in the park?

c) tell everyone in the room how stupid they both look?

9. You're training a new puppy. Despite weeks of hard work, little Fido still won't heel. Do you:
a)   patiently carry on until he understands what to do?
b)   give up and get someone else to try?
c)   exchange Fido for a hamster?

10. If you could travel in time, would you sooner spend a day:
a)   going to the moon?
b)   at a medieval banquet?
c)   watching the Battle of Gettysburg?

1.   a) 0   b) 5   c) 0
2.   a) 0   b) 5   c) 0
3.   a) 5   b) 0   c) 0
4.   a) 0   b) 0   c) 5
5.   a) 0   b) 0   c) 5
6.   a) 5   b) 0   c) 0
7.   a) 0   b) 5   c) 0
8.   a) 0   b) 5   c) 0
9.   a) 5   b) 0   c) 0
10. a) 0   b) 5   c) 0

If you scored:
40–50
You're true to your Sun sign—patient, stubborn, reliable, and sensual.

20–35
You're not *quite* true to your Sun sign. Perhaps you're learning not to be so stubborn.

0–15
You don't seem to be as true to your Sun sign as you could be. Suggestions: wear nice, soft clothes, dance every day, plant a seed and watch it grow.

GEMINI

1. You've been invited to go away for a long weekend on very short notice. It looks as though it could be fun. Do you:
a) say no and pretend you've got an exam coming up—really you're too shy?
b) say it sounds great and start packing?
c) agree to go but only because you don't want to hurt anyone's feelings?

2. You're in real trouble at school. In your interview with the principal do you:
a) try to talk your way out of it?
b) apologize and feel terribly guilty?
c) refuse to say anything until your lawyer arrives?

3. Imagine you're sitting in front of the television doing your homework. At the same time you're finishing your supper and planning the events for the coming weekend. Does this scenario:
a) sound disorganized and dreadful?
b) sound like an incredible feat of mental dexterity?
c) sound exactly like you?

4. Your report card says some wonderful things about you. However, there's always one criticism. Are you:
a) too moody?
b) too chatty?
c) too bossy?

5. The party's getting really boring. Do you:
a) go in the kitchen and start cleaning up?
b) assume it's your fault because you're feeling shy?
c) start a conversation with someone you haven't talked to before?

6. During break, one of your friends is showing everyone some new card tricks. Are you:
a) so intrigued that you want her to show you how she did the tricks?
b) so impressed that you almost believe the tricks are really magic?
c) envious of all the attention she's getting?

7. You're babysitting for a neighbor. Which of these activities are you likely to do as soon as the front door closes and you've checked that the baby's comfortable:
a) write a letter to a friend?
b) get your sketchbook and draw the sleeping baby?
c) straighten up the living room?

8. Your new boyfriend/girlfriend says she loves you. Do you:
a) become very quiet and shy?
b) think that it's a funny thing to say after only two dates?
c) plan what you'll be wearing for your wedding?

9. Your neighbor's very young children have been left at your place for a Saturday afternoon. They're playing all sorts of games. Do you:

a) join in and have a great time?
b) lock yourself in your bedroom?
c) try and make them sit down and be sensible?

10. If you were going to be remembered by the world in 100 years' time, would you like it to be for:
a) a medical breakthrough?
b) a major sporting achievement?
c) developing a new global communications network?

1. a) 0   b) 5   c) 0
2. a) 5   b) 0   c) 0
3. a) 0   b) 0   c) 5
4. a) 0   b) 5   c) 0
5. a) 0   b) 0   c) 5
6. a) 5   b) 0   c) 0
7. a) 5   b) 0   c) 0
8. a) 0   b) 5   c) 0
9. a) 5   b) 0   c) 0
10. a) 0   b) 0   c) 5

If you scored:
40–50
You're true to your Sun sign—versatile, witty, zany, and clever.

20–35
You're not *quite* true to your Sun sign. Perhaps you're learning to organize yourself a little better.

0–15
You don't seem to be as true to your Sun sign as you could be. Suggestions: buy a book, learn to say hello in five languages, have fun.

CANCER

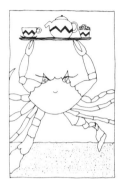

1. A close friend confides in you. She thinks she's really unattractive. Do you:
a) put your arm around her and tell her everyone thinks she's really pretty?
b) tell her she could do with a new haircut?
c) feel edgy at being put on the spot?

2. One of your friends is very nasty to you. Do you:
a) laugh it off (you never liked him/her much anyway)?
b) make out that you don't care but underneath you're really very upset?
c) have a huge blazing argument?

3. If you were suddenly given a lot of money would you:
a) go on a trip to a hundred exotic destinations?
b) buy a lovely home for you and your family?
c) make a record and pay for it yourself?

4. You're walking around the school with a gray cloud hanging over you. You overhear some friends talking about you. Are they likely to be saying:
a) "he/she can be a bit moody sometimes"?
b) "I wonder what's wrong. He/she's always so cheerful"?
c) "He/she is in trouble with the principal *again*"?

5. When you break up with your boyfriend/girlfriend are you likely to:
a)   never see that person again if you can possibly help it?
b)   keep trying to revive the relationship?
c)   make sure your ex sees you out with someone new?

6. You're looking through a magazine and you come across a picture of three cute little kittens. Do you:
a)   use the photo as part of your project on Different Breeds of the Domestic Cat?
b)   ignore it?
c)   go all mushy and wish they were in your arms so you could cuddle them?

7. In a family discussion, someone brings up a story about you when you were very young. Are you likely to:
a)   have forgotten the incident completely and feel terribly embarrassed about the conversation?
b)   remember every detail and enjoy people talking about it?
c)   dimly recall the best bits without much enthusiasm?

8. You're on a first date and you spill ice cream down your clothes. Do you:
a)   feel so awkward and embarrassed that you just want to go home?
b)   laugh about it and put some on the end of your nose as a finishing touch?
c)   carry the whole thing off as if it was a totally normal thing to do?

9. You're staying in a country cottage for your summer vacation. On the first day do you:
a)   find out what local amusements there are?
b)   make sure the cupboards are full of food and that you've got everything you need to make your stay comfortable?

c) dump your bags, say goodbye, and go off to explore the countryside?

10. If you could be a building would you choose to be:
a) a train station?
b) a hotel?
c) a factory?

1. a) 5   b) 0   c) 0
2. a) 0   b) 5   c) 0
3. a) 0   b) 5   c) 0
4. a) 5   b) 0   c) 0
5. a) 0   b) 5   c) 0
6. a) 0   b) 0   c) 5
7. a) 0   b) 5   c) 0
8. a) 5   b) 0   c) 0
9. a) 0   b) 5   c) 0
10. a) 0   b) 5   c) 0

If you scored:
40–50
You're true to your Sun sign—caring, moody, protective, and sensitive.

20–35
You're not *quite* true to your Sun sign. Perhaps you're learning not to go off in a huff so easily.

0–15
You don't seem to be as true to your Sun sign as you could be. Suggestions: make your rooms more cozy, start a photograph album, cook something special for someone you love.

LEO

1. You've been given a huge bag of chocolate bars for your birthday. Do you:
a) store them in your bedroom and take them to school, one at a time, to eat during break?
b) take them to school and hand them out to your friends?
c) have a chocolate orgy on your birthday and eat them all yourself?

2. Your best friend is giving a party. She asks you to help her with the preparations. Do you:
a) reluctantly lend a hand?
b) tell her not to throw a party unless she's capable of organizing it herself?
c) take over?

3. It's your boyfriend/girlfriend's first birthday since you've been together. Do you:
a) buy a giant birthday card, the best present you can afford, and make it a really special day?
b) remember at the last minute and quickly get something from the nearest shop?
c) get something really cheap in case you change your mind about the relationship?

4. Tim, a friend you've known for many years, is starting to get a bad reputation in the neighborhood. At school, another friend starts to say horrible things about Tim. Do you:
a) agree that Tim is going off the deep end?
b) add some extra rumors to stir things up?
c) stick up for Tim no matter what anyone says?

5. It's the end of term party. The DJ asks for someone to dance in the spotlight. Do you:
a) suddenly realize that you're dying to go to the lavatory and run out of the hall?
b) leap on to the stage and do your devastating impersonation of Prince/Madonna?
c) push your friend into the spotlight?

6. Your eight-year-old niece has just completed the most difficult computer game you've ever seen. You can only manage the first level. Do you feel:
a) so impressed that you ask her to give you lessons?
b) horribly humiliated but happy that you've got a little genius in the family?
c) so annoyed that you stop her from doing any more?

7. Your family has just won a luxury holiday in the Caribbean. Do you:
a) not tell anyone in case they get jealous?
b) modestly refer to your holiday in general conversation?
c) brag about your holiday at every available opportunity?

8. You've been told that you can't go out unless you finish your homework. Are you likely to:
a) flounce off and yell at anyone foolish enough to cross your path?
b) reluctantly agree and quietly do your work?
c) appear to agree and then secretly slip out?

9. It's exam time and you've done very little studying. Do you:
a) feel that your natural intelligence will see you through?
b) worry all night and work till breakfast?
c) cheat?

10. One holiday a genie appears and says he'll grant you a wish for the day. Would you choose:
a) a day visiting the world's mountain peaks?
b) a day in Hollywood to meet the stars?
c) a day behind the scenes in Congress?

1. a) 0   b) 5   c) 0
2. a) 0   b) 0   c) 5
3. a) 5   b) 0   c) 0
4. a) 0   b) 0   c) 5
5. a) 0   b) 5   c) 0
6. a) 0   b) 5   c) 0
7. a) 0   b) 0   c) 5
8. a) 5   b) 0   c) 0
9. a) 5   b) 0   c) 0
10. a) 0   b) 5   c) 0

If you scored:
40–50
You're true to your Sun sign—loyal, proud, generous, and bossy.

20–35
You're not *quite* true to your Sun sign. Perhaps you're learning to lead without pushing people around.

0–15
You don't seem to be as true to your Sun sign as you could be. Suggestions: join a drama group, wear lots of yellow, feel proud of your achievements.

VIRGO

1. You sneeze twice after breakfast. Do you:
a) blow your nose?
b) assume you're going to be ill, get someone to take your temperature, and retire miserably to bed?
c) accuse someone in your family of giving you a cold?

2. It's your first date. You're meeting him/her outside the movies at 6:30. Do you:
a) keep him/her waiting till 6:45 (it's not cool to arrive on time)?
b) completely forget you've arranged anything and go somewhere else?
c) get there at 6:00 in case the bus doesn't turn up or there's heavy traffic?

3. You've just bought a fantastic new jumper. When you get it home you notice a tiny mark on the inside of the arm. Do you:
a) try the jumper on immediately and forget about the mark?
b) return it to the shop and ask for another jumper in perfect condition?
c) put a mark on the other arm and pretend it's a pattern?

4. Your class has been given a very complicated technology problem to solve. You're working in groups. Do you:
a) methodically work out what you have to do, solve the problem, and tell your group?
b) try lots of different options and hope something will turn out successfully?
c) keep quiet and hope nobody notices that you haven't contributed?

5. Your elderly neighbor can't go shopping at the moment. Do you:
a) hope she doesn't ask you to get her anything?
b) try not to think about her but feel so guilty that you end up offering to help?
c) do her shopping when you can, help with her pets, and read to her from time to time?

6. A friend shows you her essay and it's full of grammatical errors. Do you:
a) point out all the mistakes?
b) read it and hand it back with a mysterious smile?
c) read it through superficially and say it's brilliant?

7. You're at a party and you've been told someone really likes you. Do you:
a) walk over, stand next to them, and try to look fascinating?
b) watch from a distance and check him/her out?
c) go straight up to him/her and ask for a dance?

8. You've just spent days making a beautiful birthday card for your best friend. As he/she opens it do you:
a) smile proudly and say how long it took you to make?
b) feel suddenly awkward in case they would have preferred a store-bought card?
c) wish you could have the card back for 24 hours because you've just seen loads of things wrong with it?

9. You've been anxious about your exams. Now they're over, you've done well and you haven't got anything to worry about do you:
a) feel fantastic?
b) know you'll probably have some problems in the future but enjoy feeling relaxed for now?
c) worry?

10. If you could be a famous person from history, which of these would you choose:
a) Florence Nightingale?
b) Napoleon Bonaparte?
c) Attila the Hun?

1. a) 0   b) 5   c) 0
2. a) 0   b) 0   c) 5
3. a) 0   b) 5   c) 0
4. a) 5   b) 0   c) 0
5. a) 0   b) 0   c) 5
6. a) 5   b) 0   c) 0
7. a) 0   b) 5   c) 0
8. a) 0   b) 0   c) 5
9. a) 0   b) 0   c) 5
10. a) 5   b) 0   c) 0

If you scored:
40–50
You're true to your Sun sign—precise, helpful, critical, and clever.

20–35
You're not *quite* true to your Sun sign. Perhaps you're learning that trying your best is sometimes good enough.

0–15
You don't seem to be as true to your Sun sign as you could be. Suggestions: tidy something up for fun, find some problems to solve, make something small and fine.

LIBRA

1. The telephone rings just as you're going out to meet your new boyfriend/girlfriend. It's someone really attractive that you met last week. Do you:
a) flirt wildly?
b) say you're really sorry but you should never have given him/her your number?
c) get flustered, pretend you're someone else, and hang up?

2. You're out shopping for a jacket. In the department store you find two jackets that suit you perfectly, but you've only got enough money for one. Do you:
a) make a quick decision and buy the first one you saw?
b) have so much difficulty in choosing that you go home empty-handed?
c) buy a hat?

3. You and your friends are having a heated argument about Melissa. Some people are saying she's a real snob, others that she's just very clever. Do you:
a) mention Melissa's good points but try and understand what the others are getting at?
b) get really into the gossip and enjoy an opportunity to cut the person down?
c) tell everyone they're being cruel and storm off?

4. You've been told to clear out your closets so that your room can be redecorated. Do you:

a) do a little every day so that your room's ready on time?

b) dump everything in the hall and let someone else sort it out?

c) put it off for so long that you're trying to empty the closets while the walls are being washed down?

5. You've been invited to a fancy costume party. Do you go as:

a) a romantic vision from history?

b) a monster from a horror movie?

c) a mailbox?

6. You want a new pair of sneakers for your birthday, but your family has got other ideas. Do you:

a) leave the ones you normally wear on the kitchen table so everyone can see how old, smelly, and small they are?

b) point out that your feet are growing quickly and you'll need a new pair soon anyway?

c) say you can't possibly go to school until you get them?

7. Your best friend is in the school play. She's not a good actress. Afterwards, do you:

a) say you really liked her costume and don't mention her acting?

b) keep changing the subject for the next few days?

c) tell her she'd be better off working backstage?

8. Would you say a good motto for life is:

a) neither a borrower nor a lender be?

b) look before you leap?

c) it's all a question of balance?

9. If you were going for a high-powered job in government, would it be in:

a)   the Treasury?
b)   the Peace Corps?
c)   the Department of Agriculture?

10. It's a gray winter's afternoon. A magic carpet appears outside your window. Do you ask it to take you to:
a)   a chocolate factory?
b)   a faraway planet so you can see the workings of an advanced civilization?
c)   a tropical rain forest so you can study the vegetation?

1.	a) 5	b) 0	c) 0
2.	a) 0	b) 5	c) 0
3.	a) 5	b) 0	c) 0
4.	a) 0	b) 0	c) 5
5.	a) 5	b) 0	c) 0
6.	a) 0	b) 5	c) 0
7.	a) 5	b) 0	c) 0
8.	a) 0	b) 0	c) 5
9.	a) 0	b) 5	c) 0
10.	a) 5	b) 0	c) 0

If you scored:
40–50
You're true to your Sun sign—reasonable, indecisive, charming, and flirtatious.

20–35
You're not *quite* true to your Sun sign. Perhaps you're finding out that you can say what you mean without *always* having to smile sweetly.

0–15
You don't seem to be as true to your Sun sign as you could be. Suggestions: do something beautiful to your room, ask someone you like to tea, remember to look at both sides of any situation.

SCORPIO

1. As you're walking home from school you see your boyfriend/girlfriend laughing and joking with someone gorgeous of the opposite sex. Are you:

a) happy that your boyfriend/girlfriend is widening his/her circle of friends?

b) so curious about the conversation that you decide to go up to them and join in?

c) mad with jealousy?

2. Your homeroom teacher says she needs some personal information from each class member for the school files. Do you:

a) resent this intrusion into your life?

b) give as much detail as possible?

c) give what you can remember and add a few jokes?

3. It's Sport's Day and you're a few points short of becoming Best All Around Performer. The final race arrives and you're completely exhausted, but you need the extra points. Do you:

a) feel it's likely that you'll lose but try your best?

b) push yourself beyond the pain barrier?

c) think nothing's worth this much agony and dawdle around the track?

4. Your friend comes to you with the most complicated emotional problem. He doesn't know what to do and he wants you to come up with a solution. Do you:

a) stare blankly at him, shrug your shoulders, and declare yourself equally puzzled?

b) penetrate to the heart of his difficulties and offer several possible alternative solutions.

c) lend a sympathetic ear but make no attempt to unravel the problem?

5. Your boyfriend/girlfriend has arrived late for a date. The excuse he/she offers is a little strange, to say the least. Do you:

a) spend the whole evening trying to get to the truth?

b) feel hurt, make an excuse, and go home?

c) just feel relieved that he/she's arrived safely?

6. Two years ago a girl in your class told you to grow up and stop being so bossy. You've ignored her ever since. She's leaving today and you've been asked to sign her farewell card. Do you:

a) sign it in a huff and wish she'd left sooner?

b) bury the hatchet and wish her the best of luck in her new school?

c) feel guilty about your behavior and buy her a box of chocolates to go with the card?

7. If you were a book would you rather be:

a) a fairy story?

b) a murder mystery?

c) a dictionary?

8. Someone in your family has obviously been reading your diary. Are you:

a) not really bothered (there wasn't anything interesting in it anyway)?

b) worried, in case they read something about themselves that might upset them?
c) furious?

9. You're on your way to school when an old lady faints in a crosswalk. Do you:
a) keep calm, get someone to stop the traffic, and do what first aid you can until help comes?
b) panic?
c) keep on going to school and let someone else help her out?

10. You're working on an experiment in the science laboratory. The bell rings for lunch and unfortunately you haven't quite finished. Do you:
a) try and clean up, forget your notes, and go to lunch?
b) tell your teacher you want to keep working through the lunch break?
c) breathe a sigh of relief since it was all going wrong anyway?

1. a) 0   b) 0   c) 5
2. a) 5   b) 0   c) 0
3. a) 0   b) 5   c) 0
4. a) 0   b) 5   c) 0
5. a) 5   b) 0   c) 0
6. a) 5   b) 0   c) 0
7. a) 0   b) 5   c) 0
8. a) 0   b) 0   c) 5
9. a) 5   b) 0   c) 0
10. a) 0   b) 5   c) 0

If you scored:
40–50
You're true to your Sun sign—analytical, jealous, strong-willed, and intense.

20–35

You're not *quite* true to your Sun sign. Perhaps you're learning to trust more people with your secrets.

0–15

You don't seem to be as true to your Sun sign as you could be. Suggestions: do some research into a mysterious subject, learn a martial art, write a passionate love song.

SAGITTARIUS

1. Your boyfriend/girlfriend asks you whether you like his/her new watch. You think it looks like a small piece of scrap metal. Do you say:

a) "Wow! What a lovely watch. It really suits you"?

b) "Yes, it looks all right—but is it accurate?"

c) "I think your watch looks like a small piece of scrap metal"?

2. You're about to go on a family summer vacation. The weather forecast describes freak gales and you've read in the paper that the hotel you'll be staying in hasn't been finished yet. Your family is wondering what to do. Are you:

a) completely dejected. You keep saying things like "We're all doomed"?
b) still looking forward to going away. You keep saying "I'm sure we'll still have loads of fun"?
c) hoping that this means the trip can be canceled and you can stay at home?

3. You're chatting with a friend in your room and you notice two flies walking down a window pane. Do you:
a) open the window and shoo them out?
b) get the fly spray?
c) bet two candies that the one on the left reaches the windowsill first?

4. Your geography project has been given top marks. When you get home, do you:
a) boast unashamedly about your achievement?
b) leave your project where someone might notice it, then act unconcerned when your high marks are discovered?
c) modestly tell your family of your mark, praise other people's work, and don't mention you came out on top?

5. On vacation you come across some wide open fields. Is your first urge to:
a) get out your sketchbook or take a photograph?
b) run through them smiling happily?
c) think about how important it is to preserve the country-side?

6. Someone in the class has asked a question and you don't think the teacher has given the correct answer. Do you:
a) keep quiet and explain things to your classmate after the lesson?
b) keep quiet in case you're wrong?
c) interrupt the teacher and explain what you think the answer should be?

7. You've been going out with your new boyfriend/girl-friend for a couple of weeks. It's getting more and more obvious that he/she likes staying in and watching TV. Do you:
a) look forward to loads more cozy evenings?
b) feel bored and twitchy because you like going out?
c) feel that you're wasting time when you could be doing something useful together?

8. You're on a school field trip. The class goes for a walk in a huge forest and you get lost. Do you:
a) feel very scared and imagine that you'll never get out?
b) sit down calmly and wait for someone to find you?
c) turn the situation into an adventure and find your way back?

9. You get together with some classmates to form a small friendly sports club that meets every Saturday. Would your job be:
a) to write and enforce the club rules?
b) treasurer?
c) to make refreshments?

10. Would your dream be to:
a) have a steady job for life?
b) travel around the world?
c) become a brain surgeon?

1.	a) 0	b) 0	c) 5
2.	a) 0	b) 5	c) 0
3.	a) 0	b) 0	c) 5
4.	a) 5	b) 0	c) 0
5.	a) 0	b) 5	c) 0
6.	a) 0	b) 0	c) 5
7.	a) 0	b) 5	c) 0
8.	a) 0	b) 0	c) 5
9.	a) 5	b) 0	c) 0
10.	a) 0	b) 5	c) 0

If you scored:
40–50
You're true to your Sun sign—optimistic, restless, opinionated and honest.

20–35
You're not *quite* true to your Sun sign. Perhaps you're learning to tell the truth without putting your foot in it.

0–15
You don't seem to be as true to your Sun sign as you could be. Suggestions: get an atlas and read it every day, involve yourself in a sport, be positive.

CAPRICORN

1. You're at a barbecue with your boyfriend/girlfriend. A rather interesting and attractive person begins to flirt with you. Do you:
a) make it very clear you're with someone else?
b) flirt back and forget about the person you came with?
c) feel flattered, begin to respond, then stop because you feel so guilty?

2. It's summer vacation and you've decided to get your bike out and go for a long ride. However, it obviously needs new brakes, new tires, etc. Do you:
a) give up the whole idea—swimming suddenly seems like much more fun?
b) try and persuade a fanatical biking friend to help you?
c) do the work yourself and enjoy getting it right?

3. There's a big family gathering. After the meal do you:
a) take your long-lost cousin for a walk?
b) feel that you ought to help out with the cleaning up and get on with it right away?
c) pretend you've got homework to do and disappear to your room?

4. It's Valentine's Day and you're dying to let a special person know how you feel. Do you:
a) send a Valentine card without signing it but make no effort to disguise your writing on the envelope?
b) send a really anonymous card?
c) send an anonymous card but get a friend to drop *big hints*.

5. You've been given a beautiful diary for your birthday. Would you:
a) put it in a drawer and forget about it?
b) use it for scrap paper?
c) write down the things you've been doing and the important dates you've got to remember?

6. You're walking down the road with your boyfriend/girl-friend and he/she keeps trying to hug and kiss you. Do you:
a) feel really awkward and try to move away?
b) enjoy this public display of affection?
c) say he/she's being silly and make a joke out of it?

7. When you get pocket money do you:
a) blow it all every week?
b) work out how much you want to save and how much you want to spend?
c) forget how much you've been given; lose some; give some away?

8. The school sweet shop, run by the students, needs someone to take charge of everything. At the moment you're helping out with the stock. Do you:
a) think that you couldn't possibly do it—you're happier taking orders?
b) know that you could do the job and volunteer yourself?
c) go for the job because you might get some time out of class?

9. You're having a meal with your best friend and his/her family. Everyone's arguing about a particular item on the news that you feel strongly about too. Would you:
a) give your opinion and expect to be taken seriously?
b) keep quiet because you don't like arguments?
c) interrupt anyone who's talking with your opinions?

10. If a good fairy at your birth had given you a special superhuman power, would it be:
a) the ability to control time?
b) invisibility?
c) X-ray vision?

1. a) 5 b) 0 c) 0
2. a) 0 b) 0 c) 5
3. a) 0 b) 5 c) 0
4. a) 0 b) 5 c) 0
5. a) 0 b) 0 c) 5
6. a) 5 b) 0 c) 0
7. a) 0 b) 5 c) 0

8. a) 0   b) 5   c) 0
9. a) 5   b) 0   c) 0
10. a) 5   b) 0   c) 0

If you scored:
40–50
You're true to your Sun sign—ambitious, dutiful, cautious, and organized.

20–35
You're not *quite* true to your Sun sign. Perhaps you're learning to have more fun without being any less hard-working and efficient.

0–15
You don't seem to be as true to your Sun sign as you could be. Suggestions: be punctual, write down things you want to do (and do them!), never give up.

AQUARIUS

1. Even though you haven't known each other for very long, your boyfriend/girlfriend is starting to insist that you meet at least twice or three times a week. Do you:
a) find all this enthusiasm flattering?
b) get very flustered and say that you need more space?
c) say you're much too busy?

2. Which one of these song titles appeals to you:
a) Rebel Rebel?
b) Sugar Sugar?
c) Mmm Mmm Mmm Mmm?

3. You've got to design the front page of a newspaper for an English project on the first flight of Concorde. Do you:
a) research the project properly and produce a detailed piece of work?
b) write about the event with the emphasis on catering?
c) call your newspaper *The Daily Feather* and write about the whole event from the point of view of the bird population around Heathrow Airport in London?

4. You've just had an awful haircut. You can hardly believe how bad it is. Do you:
a) act as if you don't care but secretly wish that you could wear a hat/wig/scarf for a month?
b) feel so upset that you insist you're not going out until your hair grows back?
c) lock yourself in the bathroom with mousse, gels, combs, and brushes until you've found a way of making it look interesting.

5. You believe very strongly in a political/environmental issue but feel frustrated because you can't change anything on your own. Do you:
a) join a local group that deals specifically with that issue?
b) feel so disheartened and powerless that you give up?
c) keep trying by yourself no matter what it takes?

6. Your family isn't very keen on your boyfriend/girl-friend because he/she's a little eccentric. Do you:
a) stop seeing him/her to keep the peace?
b) ignore them and continue your relationship?
c) ask him/her to be a bit more conventional around your family?

7. Your radio/cassette player isn't working. Do you:
a) shake it and bang it a few times and hope something reconnects?
b) work out what's wrong and see if you can fix it?
c) ask for a new one?

8. If you had limitless money to decorate your room and buy all the things you wanted to put in it would you have:
a) a huge fish tank, tropical plants, and a water bed?
b) a magnificent feather bed, dozens of pillows and cushions, and a thick pile carpet?
c) a light, spacious room furnished with every available piece of technological equipment—state of the art computers, keyboards, screens, etc.?

9. Once you've made up your mind about something are you likely to:
a) stick with your opinion until you decide it's time to change?
b) be easily persuaded to think differently?
c) change it five minutes later?

10. You've been given the opportunity to make a million dollar blockbuster film in Hollywood. Would you produce:
a) a passionate love story?
b) an intergalactic science fiction epic?
c) a comedy thriller with a superstar cast?

1. a) 0   b) 5   c) 0
2. a) 5   b) 0   c) 0
3. a) 0   b) 0   c) 5
4. a) 0   b) 0   c) 5
5. a) 5   b) 0   c) 0
6. a) 0   b) 5   c) 0
7. a) 0   b) 5   c) 0
8. a) 0   b) 0   c) 5
9. a) 5   b) 0   c) 0
10. a) 0   b) 5   c) 0

If you scored:
40–50
You're true to your Sun sign—inventive, humanitarian, rebellious, and determined.

20–35
You're not *quite* true to your Sun sign. Perhaps you're finding out that new ideas aren't always right and old ideas aren't always wrong.

0–15
You don't seem to be as true to your Sun sign as you could be. Suggestions: take up photography, join a special interest group, develop your computing skills.

PISCES

1. A friend asks you to look after his much-loved dog while he's on vacation. Your family doesn't mind at all. Do you:
a) say no because you don't want the responsibility?
b) say yes because you know it'll be fun and you'll have a lovely time?
c) say yes but let your family look after the dog during its stay?

2. It's the weekend and you've volunteered to make dinner. Do you:

a) forget till the last minute and do something quick on toast?

b) end up roping other people in to do most of the work but still take the credit?

c) find a really delicious recipe and present the meal nicely?

3. You're watching a film on television with your family when a very moving scene comes on. Do you:

a) feel your eyes fill with tears and reach for a tissue?

b) go and fix a snack because you hate the mushy parts?

c) laugh?

4. You've liked somebody for ages but have never spoken to him/her. One day he/she comes up to you and starts a conversation. Are you:

a) disappointed because he/she is really quite ordinary?

b) so excited that you can't string two words together?

c) so interested in what's being said that you forget how much you liked him/her in the first place?

5. You've been having a bath, washing your hair, and generally hogging the bathroom. Somebody knocks impatiently on the door. Do you:

a) ignore the knocking and start singing your favorite song very loudly?

b) say you'll be out in a minute and leave everything clean and tidy for the next person?

c) say you'll be out soon but get so lost in your bath-time daydream that you forget to hurry up?

6. You're feeling a bit miserable. You bump into a friend who's beaming because he's/she's just had some wonderful news. Do you:

a) immediately forget how sad you are and become as excited as your friend?

b) say you're not in the mood to talk to anyone?

c) say you're really pleased for him/her but find it impossible to smile?

7. If you were sailing around the world by yourself and only had room for one nonessential thing would you take:
a) some means of listening to music?
b) a suitcase full of computer games?
c) a huge crate of assorted sweets?

8. Although we all dream every night, do you personally think of your dreams as:
a) irregular and dull?
b) colorful, vivid, and very important to you?
c) nonexistent—you never remember having any?

9. While you're washing up you break a special plate. Do you:
a) say, "Accidents happen—it's only a plate!"?
b) leave it on the side and pretend you know nothing about it?
c) feel overwhelmed with guilt and offer to repair it or buy a new one?

10. Which of these would you rather live in:
a) a high-tech penthouse?
b) a magic castle?
c) a semidetached house in suburbia?

1. a) 0   b) 5   c) 0
2. a) 0   b) 0   c) 5
3. a) 5   b) 0   c) 0
4. a) 5   b) 0   c) 0
5. a) 0   b) 0   c) 5
6. a) 5   b) 0   c) 0
7. a) 5   b) 0   c) 0
8. a) 0   b) 5   c) 0

9. a) 0   b) 0   c) 5
10. a) 0   b) 5   c) 0

If you scored:
40–50
You're true to your Sun sign—sympathetic, impractical, idealistic, and imaginative.

20–35
You're not *quite* true to your Sun sign. Perhaps you're learning that if you work hard at your dreams they can come true.

0–15
You don't seem to be as true to your Sun sign as you could be. Suggestions: listen to music, write a poem, go swimming.

IF YOU WANT TO KNOW
MORE...

If you want to know more about your birth chart or more about astrology in general there are many places you can contact. Having a personal consultation with a professional astrologer is the best way of learning about your birth chart, but this costs more than getting a computerized birth chart analysis. Contact the associations noted here to locate a qualified astrologer or computer analysis service.

American Federation of Astrologers (AFA)
P.O. Box 22040
Tempe, AZ 85285-2040
Tel: 602-838-1751
Local associations and individuals in 47 countries interested in the advancement of astrology through research and education. Conducts astrological exams of persons interested in the field. *Today's Astrologer* monthly.

Association for Astrological Networking (AFAN)
8306 Wilshire Blvd., No. 537
Beverly Hills, CA 90211
Seeks to provide accurate and professional image of astrology to the public and media. Serves as a link between astrologers and the community.

Friends of Astrology (FA)
535 Woodside Ave.
Hinsdale, IL 60521
Tel: 708-654-4737
Seeks to raise the standards of astrology through scientific

research and educational programs. *Friends of Astrology Bulletin*, monthly. Contains astrological lessons, book reviews, and zodiac sign and monthly lunar forecasts.

There are many books on astrology available at your local library and in bookstores. Here are a few good ones:

Astrology: A Guide to the Signs (illus.). Andrews & McMeel. 1992. 80 p.

Astrology for Beginners: An Easy Guide to Understanding & Interpreting Your Chart. by William W. Hewitt. Llewellyn Publications, 1991. 304 p.

How to Chart Your Horoscope by Max Heindel. Wilshire, 1978.

Pocket Dictionary of Astrological Terms by Gayle Bachicha. Tickerwick, 1994. 64 p.

Stephen Arroyo's Chart Interpretation Handbook: Guidelines for Understanding the Essentials of the Birth Chart. Jerilynn Marshall, ed. CRCS Publications, CA, 1989. 184 p.